M000105232

FRIENDSHIPS
OF
FAITH

A SHARED STUDY OF HEBREWS

EDNA ELLISON

NEW HOPE
PUBLISHERS
Gospel-Centered. Missions-Driven.

New Hope® Publishers
P. O. Box 12065
Birmingham, AL 35202-2065
NewHopeDigital.com
New Hope Publishers is a division of WMU®.

The Library of Congress has cataloged the earlier edition as follows:

Ellison, Edna
    Friendships of Faith: a shared study of Hebrews/Edna Ellison.
    p. cm.
    ISBN 1-56309-762-1 (pbk.)
    1.   Bible. N.T. Hebrews—Criticism, interpretation, etc. 1. Title.
    BS2775.52.E44 2003
    227'.8707—dc21

                         2003007820

Cover Designer: Kay Chin Bishop

ISBN-10: 1-59669-362-2
ISBN-13: 978-1-59669-362-3

N134105 · 0213 · 3M1

Table of Contents

UNIT 5: *My Sacrifice of Faith*

UNIT 6: *I'm Better, Not Bitter*

Introduction

OFTEN CALLED A "RIDDLE BOOK," Hebrews is a puzzle. No one can be sure who wrote it or exactly to whom it was written. Though you can't know everything you wish about this book, here's what you can know as you study day by day.

The Hebrews were the descendants of Abraham. At times they were called *children of Israel* (Israel is another name for Jacob, Abraham's grandson). They were also called *Israelites, God's chosen people, Jews,* or the *Jewish nation.*

Many Jews in New Testament times still spoke Hebrew or Aramaic, although the New Testament was written in Greek (*Koine,* or common Greek) and later translated into English. Hebrews is a letter, perhaps written just before A.D. 70, from a Christian to other Jewish Christians—to exhort them and encourage them (read Hebrews 13:22). Just as you study this book with a good friend, you can imagine the Christian who wrote it encouraging his friends through this letter. As we study the verses in this Bible book, we will refer to the author as "Christian," since we don't know his name.

We do know that Christian was an encourager who pointed people to the Lordship of Jesus Christ. In his letter to the Hebrews, he unfolds for you the truth: Jesus is all you need. You can have a personal relationship with the Lord of the universe, who is your wonderful high priest, the all-powerful, sovereign ruler, yet the personal, compassionate Messiah who cares for you in a special way! What a Savior!

You can be assured the writer was inspired by God to write this letter, and that God can speak to you through these words. Listen to His still, small voice as you read each verse. Ask His blessing on your efforts to find Him as you study.

Hebrews is sometimes called "the Book of Better Things" since it compares Jesus to past religions, rites, and ceremonies. It points to a better covenant (a new covenant, also called a new testament) between us and our Lord, Jesus Christ. Better or superior is used 15 times in the letter.

In his introduction to the Book of Hebrews in *The Message,* Eugene Peterson says Hebrews is "written for 'too religious' Christians, for 'Jesus-and' Christians," for those who have the mistaken idea that we must believe in "Jesus-and-angels, or Jesus-and-Moses, or Jesus-and-priesthood."

As you study Hebrews with a friend, by yourself, or with a group, take a hard look at yourself. What are your add-ons? Do you believe in Jesus alone for salvation, or do you believe in Jesus-and-education, Jesus-and-cleanliness, Jesus-and-your political party, or Jesus-and-"being good" to get you to heaven? These are good questions to consider as you read.

Peterson says, "The focus becomes clear and sharp again: God's action in Jesus. And we are free once more for the act of faith, the one human action in which we don't get in the way but on the Way."

Will you join me as we study Hebrews together? It's a book to discuss, decipher, and digest. Will you listen to the words of Christian as he encourages you in your walk with Christ? In a deeper sense, will you listen to God as He guides you through His Word?

A friend in Phoenix, Daisy Hepburn, says, "Today God's people are over-challenged and under-enabled." My aim in this Bible study is to challenge you—but not to over-challenge you without enabling you. I hope you will hear not my drawling voice, but God's eternal voice calling you to action as you grow to know Him better. I pray that He will put His laws in your mind and write them on your heart (Hebrews 8:10); and as you absorb them, they will become guiding principles enabling you to serve Him better.

How to Use This Book

As you pick up this book and scan its pages, you may be seeking God's will for your life. Hebrews, a New Testament letter, has much to say about seeking God through Jesus Christ. This book will lead you step-by-step, verse-by-verse through the Hebrew letter to draw closer to Him.

You will find at the beginning of the study of each chapter of Hebrews (not necessarily each unit in this book) a poem summarizing the chapter. I hope this lyrical poetry will be a spiritual blessing to your heart, something to read aloud to others, as well as a refreshing pause of anticipation before each chapter. You will also find extra Bible reading following appropriate Scriptures, to help you in a deeper walk with God than this study offers.

This book is designed as a two-by-two Bible study so two people may share their ideas after they read these verses in Hebrews. Written in second person, it can easily be used as a personal devotional to study by yourself, at your own pace, in your quiet time with God. It is also designed as a six-week Bible study for a small group of adults or teens (five days in each of six units). May God bless you as you study Hebrews, the solid food or meat of the gospel for maturing Christians, rather than babies' milk of infant Christians (Hebrews 5:12–14). May you find deep truth in easy reading!

UNIT 1:
Jesus, My Shining Example

HEBREWS WASTES NO TIME with fluff at the beginning of the first chapter. From the first verse, you will be led to focus on Jesus alone. Christian—the name we'll use for the writer, since we don't know his name—will help you explore numerous possibilities for religious experiences; but then he discounts all of them and points us to Jesus—Jesus the Son, Jesus the high-and-lifted-up, Jesus the Creator, Jesus the miracle worker, and Jesus your precious brother. Godly woman, you will find in this unit how to quit whining (as we all do) and find God's personal plan for your life as you follow the shining example in the Son. You'll also find help when you're afraid, and experience the oil of joy.

Won't you enter into focus and fellowship with Him now? Prepare your heart to receive spiritual sustenance, a key word in this unit. Ready? Let's begin!

STUDY 1 *Father and Son*
HEBREWS 1:1–8

Take turns reading the stanzas of the poem. Circle words you think will be themes or topics in this study. Share with you study friend your anticipation and expectations.

Hebrews 1
In olden days God spoke to hearts
At many times, in various ways.
Now through His Son the Word imparts
The truth to those who sing His praise!

Let all the angels worship Him!
God laid foundations of the earth!
His throne in heav'n makes all else dim!
He gave His Son a sacred birth!

We gain salvation through the Son:
God loved us so . . . His Son then died,
. . . Loves us so much His angels run
To serve us here on earth so wide.

The minist'ring spirits sent to serve
The saints who gain salvation's prize;
And men and women who now kneel . . .
Commune with Jesus, then to rise.

—EDNA M. ELLISON, © 2002

Begin this study on your knees. Pray for direction as you study, asking God to give you insight and heart-sight to His Word.

Fulfilling God's Plan

Awesome! Christian (the name we are using for the writer of Hebrews) begins by telling his friends, the Hebrews, "We have it! Salvation. We have Him! God's Son. We have our high priest! Jesus. We don't have to be a slave to rituals any more! He is our salvation."

As he encourages the struggling band of Jewish, or Hebrew, Christians, much like your friends' text messages and online notes may encourage you today, he begins by reminding them of the revelation of Jesus, which is far superior to the wisdom of the Pharisees and other Jewish leaders in the past. Listen as He speaks truth to you:

"In the past God spoke to our forefathers through the prophets at many times and in various ways, but in these last days he has spoken to us by his Son, whom he appointed heir of all things, and through whom he made the universe."—Hebrews 1:1–2

⤝ FRIEND TO FRIEND ⤞

According to Hebrews 1:1–2, when did God speak to the Hebrew forefathers?

When did He speak through Jesus?

What do you think "last days" means?

How do you hear that phrase used today?

If you had read these words in the first century, what would you have believed about Jesus' power?

How would these verses change your motives for listening to Jesus?

Share your answers with your study friend.

Food for Thought

Years ago, a fellow teacher at the high school where I worked, Cathy, told me this story. On a short trip in the car one weekend, she became hungry. Looking at signs to nearby towns, she remembered a wonderful fast-food restaurant a few miles down the road. Cathy didn't want to get the children's hopes up, so she asked her husband, "Do you think we could get some sustenance in Newberry?" She thought her children wouldn't know the word sustenance. Her husband agreed it was a good place to stop. Their children had a great time, delighted to get a burger and fries.

A few months later, as they drove down the same highway, their pre-schooler, Leigh, shouted, "I want sustenance! Let's get sustenance again!"

As you enter this study, look for a definition of sustenance. May God sustain you through the six units of this Bible study. May He feed you daily as you feast on His Word. In Hebrews, Christian is drawing a demarcation line: Jesus' birth changed the world for all time. In fact, He changed time. Even today we measure our calendars by whether a date is B.C. (before Christ) or A.D. (anno Domini, in the year of our Lord). Biblical scholars of all generations have tried to determine the time of the last of the "last days." However, Hebrews does not focus on such controversies. No matter what you hear about the end of the world tomorrow, in this century, or in the next millennium, remember, when Christian speaks of "last days" in Hebrews, he points us to Jesus, who changed time forever!

❧ FRIEND TO FRIEND ❧

Have your children, like Cathy's, ever surprised you by understanding words you were disguising? Share with your study friend.

How would you define "sustenance"?

How does it relate to your spiritual needs now?

In the Light of His Glory and Grace

In Old Testament days, God spoke to ancestors of the early Church through prophets, wise men who discerned God's will. Christian points to a better way: God's Son. As you read Hebrews 1:3, circle descriptive words for the Son:

> "The Son is the radiance of God's glory and the exact representation of his being, sustaining all things by his powerful word. After he had provided purification for sins, he sat down at the right hand of the Majesty in heaven."

❧ FRIEND TO FRIEND ❧

Share your circled phrases with your study friend.

Verse 3 gives two descriptive phrases for the Son: "radiance of God's glory," and "representation of his being." It also lists three things the Son does.

He:
1. Sustains all things,
2. Provides purification, and
3. Sits in heaven.

According to *Webster's* dictionary, *radiant* means "vividly bright and shining" like the sun (or the Son!). It also means "marked by or expressive of love, confidence, or happiness." Both definitions describe Jesus. The Son is the radiance of God's glory—He is the radiance; He is the glory. Notice the wording here: He is *the,* not *an,* exact representation of His being. He's the one and only. To whom does the phrase "his being," refer? If you believe the word *His* is referring to God, you're correct. Jesus is God! God incarnate, in the flesh. And as the Creator, He is capable of providing purification for you and me. He is the glory—splendor, magnificence, beauty—of God in heaven, where He sits today.

Did you notice the word *sustaining*? What sustains you? Like Cathy's story at the beginning of this chapter, you can find sustenance . . . but how do you receive it? How about a comforting arm on your shoulder (from a mom, husband, friend, aunt, grandmother, etc.)? How about church work or church fellowship? Shopping? Chocolate?

❧ FRIEND TO FRIEND ❧

Share with your study friend where you find sustenance from day to day to keep you going.

A New Theme: Better Things

Hebrews 1:4 explains the Son's place: "So he became as much superior to the angels as the name he has inherited is superior to theirs." You may see a four-way parallel that reminds you of a math fraction: Jesus is to the angels as His name is to angel's names (He's above them). You can represent this not with an equal sign but with a superior ("greater than") sign:

Jesus	>	Angels
Jesus' name	>	Angels' names

Power of the Son

You can almost hear Christian shouting to the readers of Hebrews: Son-ship! Sunship! That's God's theme here. Jesus deserves to be above the angels; there's almighty power in Him, even in His name! He illustrates:

> "For to which of the angels did God ever say, 'You are my Son; today I have become your Father'? Or again, 'I will be his Father, and he will be my Son'? And again, when God brings his firstborn into the world, he says, 'Let all angels worship him'" (Hebrews 1:5–6).

Luke records the worshipful words the angels proclaimed the night of Jesus' birth: "Glory to God in the highest, and on earth peace to men" (Luke 2:14). Even the angels fall at His feet, taking their places under His lordship. Angels acknowledge Jesus is lifted up—in the highest position! Luke 2:20 brings the end of the Bethlehem story: "The shepherds returned, glorifying and praising God for all the things they had heard and seen." On that holy night, the angels and humans praised Jesus, God's Son. Take a moment now to praise God for sending His Son into your life.

Permanence of the Son

Not only is Jesus superior in power to the angels, but also He is superior in His permanence: "In speaking of the angels he says, 'He makes his angels winds, his servants flames of fire' " (Hebrews 1:7). Winds and flames are temporal—here one minute and gone the next—just as people and even angels are; but Jesus lasts forever. I like Joni Eareckson Tada's explanation of John 20:19, when Jesus, after His death, suddenly appeared to the disciples behind closed doors: the walls He came through were not permanent, but Jesus was. His resurrected body was not shadowy or ghostly, but the material of the walls was! They melted away when faced with His solid presence. Because of His righteousness, He has a permanent place in heaven, on the throne: "But about the Son he says, 'Your throne, O God, will last for ever and ever, and righteousness will be the scepter of your kingdom'" (Hebrews 1:8).

❧ FRIEND TO FRIEND ❧

What do you think "righteousness will be the scepter" means? Share your circled phrases with your study friend.

a) Scepters that kings carry are useful and right.
b) A scepter is assurance of goodness.
c) Goodness and purity of the divine Son give him eternal authority.
d) A magic wand, like a fairy godmother carries, is good to have, for three wishes.

Touch My Heart, Lord Jesus
O, Jesus, I want Your throne to last forever in my heart. I want my will to be Yours. Come in and be the Ruler, the King of my life. You are my sustenance! Let me live up to the quality of "righteousness," which is Your scepter. I dedicate this hour, this day, my whole life to you, my permanent Friend. Amen.

STUDY 2 *Favored by Him, My Personal Plan*
HEBREWS 1:9–14

A WOMEN'S GROUP IN MY SMALL HOMETOWN asked me to speak at a YMCA dinner one Tuesday night. I had written several devotionals for my church, and selected one to use. That weekend I asked God to anoint His

Word and to anoint me to share it. I looked over the devotionals, and, to my surprise, none of them made sense. I searched the Scriptures for another message. Nothing. Even when I found Bible verses underlined, nothing seemed acceptable. Tuesday afternoon I was desperate. I begged God for direction. As I scanned the Bible, Isaiah 61:1 seemed to jump off the page!

Wow! I thought, *I'd better look at these verses.*

"The Spirit of the Sovereign Lord is on me, because the Lord has anointed me to . . . bind up the brokenhearted, . . . to comfort all who mourn, and provide for those who grieve . . . to bestow on them a crown of beauty instead of ashes, the oil of gladness instead of mourning, and a garment of praise instead of a spirit of despair."

—Isaiah 61:1–3

Lord, I'm not going to speak on mourning. Bummer!

"I'm anointing you to talk about being brokenhearted."

I don't know anything about brokenness. I'm the joy girl. Let me talk about Philippians 4.

"How about Isaiah 61?"

I could wax eloquent about Philippians 4:13, "I can do everything through him who gives me strength," or Philippians 4:19, "My God will meet all your needs according to his glorious riches in Christ Jesus."

"How about Isaiah 61? Bind up the brokenhearted."

I don't know anything about being brokenhearted.

"Not true. You know everything about it. Your pride refuses to admit it. Tell them how much it hurts to lose a love."

And expose my heartache to the world? Never.

"Not 'never'. . . 'nevertheless.'"

Nevertheless . . . even if I'm uncomfortable . . . I guess I could say something about brokenness. . . .

Words flowed for a devotional speech outline. I wrote it down and dressed hurriedly so I wouldn't be late.

On the way to speak, a bad case of cold feet seized me. I begged God for my favorite, Philippians 4. I whined, "Lord, don't humiliate me like this. It's hard to be obedient. Why Isaiah 61?"

No answer.

I arrived late, and as soon as I entered, leaders ushered me to the podium, where I laid it all out. I told of hardships after my beloved husband died and my double-broken heart after a lost relationship. I added a feeble sentence about how God had sustained me through the heartbreak, and without speaking with anyone, I rushed out the door.

On the way home, I said, "Lord, I don't understand why You humiliated me. What good did it do? I admitted heartbreak—for You—but I'm not happy!"

The next day I learned from a fellow teacher at the high school that one of her adult night-school students had a miracle story. I was not interested. The student's fiancé had rejected her the day before and asked for his ring. This rejection was the last in a life of rejection from her mother, siblings, ex-husband, and even her nine-year-old son. She had decided to commit suicide.

Pretending to go to night school, she went to the Y for a membership to console her son after her death. As she walked out to swallow sleeping pills, she heard a voice: "If you are the most brokenhearted woman in the world . . ." (*That's me,* she thought.) "Jesus is the answer. He loves you. He can restore your happiness." (I was the one speaking those words, in the Y room where I was the reluctant speaker.)

She later told her teacher, "I slipped into a backseat, and Jesus saved me, not just from suicide last night, but for all eternity! I asked Him into my heart!"

Oh, God's mercy was tender. He allowed me to know that my humiliation made a difference—even helped save a life! Except for His mercy, I'd be *still* whining, "What good did that do, Lord? I don't like being obedient!"

๛ FRIEND TO FRIEND ๛

Share with your study friend your needs for righteousness and obedience. Pray for each other.

I think with an earthly view; God thinks with a spiritual view. He looks on you and me with favor; He anoints us to share in His kingdom, to become part of His plan.

Let's focus today on Jesus' anointing, a sign of His kingdom. As you study, look for qualities of a spiritual rather than an earthly kingdom. Ask God to show you His righteousness and His personal plan for you.

Christian (our name for the writer of Hebrews) says, "You have loved righteousness and hated wickedness; therefore God, your God, has set you above your companions by anointing you with the oil of joy" (Hebrews 1:9).

❧ FRIEND TO FRIEND ❧

To whom is "you" referring in verse 9? (See v. 8.)

Who are the "companions"?

What two things should *you* do in order for God to set *you* above your companions?

Discuss these questions with your study friend.

Jesus is not only the radiance, glory, and the shining Son who brings "better things" (Study 1), but He is also the shining example for you. As the holder of great righteousness, or right-ness, He can show you how to live a good life. He was more righteous than His companions (the 12 disciples and other friends) when He lived on earth, and even more righteous than angels! If He is your personal example, you can follow Him in two ways: (1) love righteousness and (2) hate wickedness. He will give you the sustenance to do these things . . . forever.

Remember these words in Hebrews 1:8? "Your throne will last forever" has been spoken at kings' coronations for centuries. In England today, "Long live the Queen!" is a popular cry. Yet you know monarchs won't live forever. Ancient priests anointed kings with oil before they sat on the holy throne. Even today we treasure oil and use it in dedications as well as in cosmetics, cooking, and medicines.

Now look at the last phrase in verse 9. What is the oil of joy? Could it be olive oil, peanut oil, or motor oil?

❧ FRIEND TO FRIEND ❧

How do you use oil?

The Oil of Joy

If you guessed this oil is olive oil, you are right. The Hebrews used it as fuel as well as an anointing balm. Early in their history, God said to Moses, "Command the Israelites to bring you clear oil of pressed olives for the light so that the [tabernacle] lamps may be kept burning continually. . . . This is to be a lasting ordinance for the generations to come" (Leviticus 24:1, 3). Also, priests used that olive oil and a special blend of spices to anoint the ark and other items in the tabernacle. God said, "This is to be my sacred anointing oil for the generations to come" (Exodus 30:31). The oil of joy can sustain you today.

Following His praise of the Son in Hebrews 1:9, Christian continues in verses 10–11: "He also says, 'In the beginning, O Lord, you laid the foundations of the earth, and the heavens are the work of your hands. They will perish, but you remain; they will all wear out like a garment.'"

⚘ FRIEND TO FRIEND ⚘

Write your definition of the "oil of joy." Share your thoughts with your study friend.

A Closet Full of Old Clothes

This week I cleaned out a closet. Since I've lost weight, I decided to try on a few of the two-sizes-too-small garments. I was sad to find the elastic deteriorated, the fabric worn thin, and the threads weak from disuse.

Look closely at the end of Hebrews 1:11. What or who is "they"?
a) Jesus' companions
b) The earth and the heavens
c) God's hands

⚘ FRIEND TO FRIEND ⚘

Discuss with your study friend how many items you have in your closet that don't fit. How does your closet reflect your spiritual life?

Scholars disagree, but it seems that "they" in verse 11 is referring to Jesus' companions on earth (v. 9). He continues: "You will roll them up like a robe; like a garment they will be changed. But you remain the same, and your years will never end" (Hebrews 1:12). Jesus is immortal and eternal; we are mortal and as transient as a vapor.

You and I Have a Guardian Angel . . .

This study ends with an interesting spiritual idea: guardian angels. In the movie classic *High Society,* Bing Crosby and Grace Kelly sang, "For you and

I have a guardian angel on high, with nothing to do but to give to you and to give to me love forever true." Christian compares Jesus to angels in verse 13: "To which of the angels did God ever say, 'Sit at my right hand until I make your enemies a footstool for your feet'?" The silent answer is "None of them." God said that only to Jesus. [Extra reading: Psalm 110:1] Then He says a remarkable thing in verse 14: "Are not all angels ministering spirits sent to serve those who will inherit salvation?"

Who are "those who will inherit salvation"? You, if you are a Christian (have repented of wrongdoing and have accepted Jesus as your personal Savior). Hallelujah! The shining Jesus loves you so much He sends angels to minister to you!

⊰ FRIEND TO FRIEND ⊱

Have you known anyone who believed an angel was a ministering spirit to him or her? Share with your study friend.

Touch My Heart, Lord Jesus
O God, touch me with the oil of joy, with lasting happiness. O my example, I desire to be set apart from my companions, always loving righteousness and hating wickedness. May my joy flow into the lives of others, fulfilling Your plan for me as I reflect the light of the Son. Thank You for blessing me in ways I'll never understand. Amen.

STUDY 3 *Pay Attention to His Signs*
HEBREW 2:1–10

Hebrews 2
God's miracles He gives, alone,
And gifts according to His will,
Point to the Christ, who left the throne,
Came lower than the angels . . . still

My heart leaps out when I look up,
He's crowned with glory, hope, and grace!
I see my Lord, my Brother's cup
As I, when tempted, glimpse His face.

My friend, my sister—brother, too—
We're slaves because Death makes us fear.
You see His eyes? What He can do?
Set free! We're safe when He is near!

Because He suffered on the cross,
And just like us was tempted, too,
He'll take our hand, lead us across,
To shores of heaven, bright and new!

—EDNA M. ELLISON, © 2002

Did you ever memorize Mark 12:30? "Love the Lord your God with all your heart and with all your soul and with all your mind and with all your strength." I have no problem loving God with all my heart and soul. He knows I am totally sold out to Him, with everything I have. For years I have also loved Him with all my strength. I've spent 16-hour days on disaster relief feeding lines; I've taught in a South American seminary with my sweat pouring and mosquitoes biting. On Sunday mornings, I've rushed to get children ready, wiping spit-up off my dress while ironing a fresh baby outfit, running into the church with a purse and diaper bag flying behind me, my mouth stuffed with my Sunday School book, sailing in with my notes to teach a Bible study, then dashing down the hall, taking my jacket off to don a choir robe, singing my heart out for another 35 minutes, and finally rushing back to the nursery and assorted classes, picking up children for the ride home, only to hit the ground running, putting the finishing touches on the biggest lunch of the week. Whew! I know what it is to serve the Lord with all my strength.

The problem I have is serving the Lord with all my mind. OK, I admit it: I have a problem with my mind. It just won't work the way I wish it would! It forgets the most important things I've entrusted to it, goes to sleep reading the Bible, and wanders during the pastor's sermon. Worse than that, it's never alert to witnessing opportunities. God must speak to me loud and clear before I get it! Sometimes I don't get it until hours later. I always think of magnificent things I should have said or done, but at the opportune moment, my brain drones on idle. You know those hospital machines that measure brain activity? Mine often measures a straight line! The words of Hebrews 2:1 were meant for me! "We must pay more careful attention, therefore, to what we have heard, so that we do not drift away." The next verses explain: "For if the message spoken by angels was binding, and every violation and disobedience received its just punishment, how shall we escape if we ignore such a great salvation? This salvation, which was first announced by the Lord, was confirmed to us by those who heard him" (Hebrews 2:2–3).

These verses call me to attention. This is the most serious passage in the second chapter of Hebrews. It contains several important truths: First, angels, God's messengers, spoke the message. Second, this is the message: every violation and disobedience will receive just punishment. Third, if that warning is true, how shall we escape if we ignore salvation? Fourth, the Lord was the first to announce salvation. And fifth, those who heard Him confirmed that salvation was real. In the third idea, Christian implies these things: (a) the warning is true, (b) the punishment is just, (c) we have a way to escape punishment, (d) the way is to accept salvation rather than ignore it, and (e) this salvation is great!

❧ FRIEND TO FRIEND ❧

Who spoke the message?

What was the message?

Does Christian (our Hebrews writer) assume or not assume the message was binding?

Share your ideas with your study friend.

What amazing truth! These two verses contain the heart of the gospel. Jesus the Son, the righteous One, the shining example, and King of kings, announced the plan of salvation: that He would die as a sacrifice for our sins and that His sacrifice would take the place of our punishment for violating God's law and for our disobedience—in short, our sins. If we accept salvation—that is, acknowledge that Jesus is the Son of God, repent, and trust Him alone for our salvation or impunity—then we can follow others who have heard Christ and confirmed this truth; we can join them in heaven for eternity.

❧ FRIEND TO FRIEND ❧

Have you paid attention as God has led you in this study?

Do you think you have accepted the good news that Jesus is our salvation from punishment?

If so, share with your friend the experience of your decision.

If not, have you . . .

a) absentmindedly ignored the truth, because you'd never thought about it

b) purposefully ignored the truth, because it made no sense intellectually

c) turned your back on Jesus because bad things had happened to you and you felt you couldn't trust Him

d) had too much pride to accept the truth of salvation

Can you think of things you have done that need forgiveness?

If you would like to commit your life to Jesus, pray this prayer now:

O God, I know I'm a sinner. I truly regret my disobedience. Forgive me, Lord. I want to turn from that life and live for You. Come into my heart right now; live within me. I trust You to save me, to help me live righteously, and then to take me to heaven to live with You for eternity. Thank You, God, in Jesus' name, amen.

Will Wonders Never Cease!

Not only did Jesus announce the gospel (good news of salvation), and the believers who heard Him confirmed that it was true, but someone else testified to it. Find in Hebrews 2:4 who testified to it, and how: "God also testified to it by signs, wonders and various miracles, and gifts of the Holy Spirit distributed according to his will."

Christian continues the "better things" theme by showing how Jesus compares to angels:

"It is not to angels that he has subjected the world to come, about which we are speaking. But there is a place where someone has testified: 'What is man that you are mindful of him, the son of man that you care for him? You made him a little lower than the angels; you crowned him with glory and honor and put every-thing under his feet.' In putting everything under him, God left nothing that is not subject to him. Yet at present we do not see everything subject to him" (Hebrews 2:5–8).

Verse 5 begins by saying it is not to angels that God has subjected the world to come; that is, angels will not be in charge of heaven. The implication is that Jesus will be ruler over heaven, as part of the Godhead. "There is a place" seems to point to earth, not heaven. The quote, "What is man . . ." is from Psalm 8:3–5. The author of the Book of Psalms recognized that God was mindful of puny man; God's *infinite* mind, far above your *finite* one, is full of concern. He cared about David; He cares about you, every detail of your life. He cared about the Son of Man, a name Jesus often used to refer to Himself.

Wait a minute! Do these verses say Jesus is lower, not higher than the angels? Read carefully. Aha! These verses say that all humans are lower than the angels, though they are crowned with glory and honor and God put everything under their feet. Genesis 1:27–28 explains: "So God created man in his own image . . . male and female he created them. God blessed them and said . . . 'Fill the earth and subdue it.' " He gave humans control overall animals and plants on earth. Hebrews 2:5–8 also indicates that the Son of Man was made lower than the angels too; He humbled Himself to become a human, to provide salvation for us, in the flesh.

✤ FRIEND TO FRIEND ✤

List the ways God testified to Jesus' power to save us.

How has God worked miraculously in your life?

What do David's words teach you about God? Yourself?

Share with your study friend.

The Glory and Honor of Jesus

Christian continues: "But we see Jesus, who was made a little lower than the angels, now crowned with glory and honor because he suffered death, so that by the grace of God he might taste death for everyone" (Hebrews 2:9). I am so grateful that Jesus loved me so much He "made himself nothing, taking the very nature of a servant . . . in human likeness. . . . and became obedient to death" (Philippians 2:6–7). The worst sin you can commit is to ignore Him. To be satisfied, even defiant, about being apart from Him is to flirt with everlasting death.

Look again at verse 8: "Yet at present we do not see everything subject to him." Are you subject to Jesus? Do you consciously come under His authority? Pray that you will move close to Him, under His wing.

Author! Author!

Christian introduces the theme of *glory* in Hebrews 2:10—"In bringing many sons to glory, it was fitting that God, for whom and through whom everything exists, should make the author of their salvation perfect through suffering." I believe "bringing sons to glory" means bringing you to know Jesus; bringing you to heaven. When I was a girl we sang, "I've got a home in Gloryland that outshines the sun." I depend on God's providing my place in heaven. How about you?

The author of salvation is Almighty God, who suffered through His Son, Jesus, who is made a perfect sacrifice through suffering. Hallelujah! We will follow His signs to heaven.

✑ FRIEND TO FRIEND ✑

Why did Jesus humble Himself and come to earth?

How Is Jesus "now crowned with glory and honor" (Hebrews 2:9)?

Share with your study friend.

Touch My Heart, Lord Jesus
Lord, I stand humbled before You. I see You, O Jesus, as I look for signs of Your love. Thank You for leaving the glory of heaven to come to a sinful earth and even die for me, as a perfect sacrifice. May my heart be acceptable to You. Help me to share as Christian did in his day, to confirm in others that You are King of kings and King of my heart. Amen.

STUDY 4 *Blessed Be the Name*

HEBREWS 2:11–13

HAVE YOU EVER attended a family reunion when you were ashamed of a family member? Aw, come on—admit it. Every family has someone they're not proud to claim. All of us have a Goofy Greg, Witchy Winnie, Snooty Snyder, Druggy Doug, Sloppy Sally, Egghead Edgar, or Dumb Dora. I have several family members who are strange, crazy, eccentric, or just plain weird! We have a saying in our family: "We ain't right," to account for those of us who just don't have it all together!

Now here's the good news: we may not have it all together, but Jesus does. What's more, He accepts us just the way we are, with all our faults and eccentricities. It's all in the family. Christian, our name for the Hebrews writer, says, "Both the one who makes men holy and those who are made holy are of the same family. So Jesus is not ashamed to call them brothers" (Hebrews 2:11).

Tear this verse down into its appropriate parts. The one: Jesus. Those who are made holy: us. We can be of the same family because we are claimed by Jesus Himself! He is not ashamed of us, even though we are sinners.

The Family Name

Notice the sidebar question that asks you not to mention the names of your strange family members, to prevent embarrassment or to avoid gossip. However, Jesus is able to mention your name as He claims you as His family member. Your name has been cleared! Verse 11 reminds me of Haggai 2:23—"'I will make you like my signet ring [stamped with my initial], for I have chosen you,' declares the Lord Almighty." Just as blond hair, a pug nose, or a strong chin line stamps you as a member of your family, God has chosen you as a child of God. Jesus claims you as a brother or sister! Paul says in Romans 8:15–17: "You received the Spirit of sonship. And by him we cry, 'Abba, Father.' The Spirit himself testifies with our spirit that we are God's children. Now if we are children, then we are heirs—heirs of God and co-heirs [or "joint-heirs" (KJV)] with Christ." As an adopted sister, you can even have the family name: *Christian*. Spend a moment now singing "Blessed Be the Name" if you know that hymn. Now you can say in your heart: blessed be the name—the family name, that is.

❧ FRIEND TO FRIEND ❧

Do you have a few strange family members?

Without mentioning names, share their characteristics with your study friend.

Do you believe "blood is thicker than water"? How do you show your family loyalty despite differences?

1. Who is the "one who makes men holy" mentioned in verse 11?

2. Who are "those who are made holy"?

3. How can we be of the same family?

Declaring His Name and Singing

Christian quotes Jesus: "He says, 'I will declare your name to my brothers; in the presence of the congregation I will sing your praises.' . . . And again he says, 'Here am I, and the children God has given me'" (Hebrews 2:12–13). I love to hum the chorus, "I'm so glad I'm a part of the family of God." Rejoice with me as children of Almighty God, the Great I AM!

It's one thing to claim your awkward relatives, but another to declare their kinship in the presence of others. I remember not wanting to claim my little brother, Jimmy, when we both went to a party with other teens. I was mortified when I was randomly paired with him during a game. Then I looked at him and realized that he was more embarrassed than I was. I saw how much I liked him—loved him—and invited him to play on our team. I was proud of my little brother. Acknowledging him in public was a hard hurdle to overcome!

Don't you find it's easier to claim your children than your brothers and sisters? The truth is that your children are often extensions of yourself, your own flesh and blood, with your DNA characteristics. Perhaps your siblings have a history of rivalry within your family, and it's harder to love them. Is today the day you should make something right with a sister or brother—or even a child? Maybe there is a hurt from the past you just couldn't forgive. Maybe the hurt included embarrassment, or money taken out of your pocket, or hardship of the worst kind as a result of the broken relationship. You may have even said, "I'll forgive, but I'll never forget."

If you know the chorus "I'm so glad I'm a part of the family of God," share it with your study friend.

Do you ever feel you do not deserve to be in God's family? Discuss what you've gained by being in the family of God.

Were you ever embarrassed by your father's car, your mother's old-fashioned dress, or your brother or sister's behavior?

Discuss with your study friend.

Consider this: if Jesus could forgive you, accepting all you've done that you know is not honest, loving, or moral, do you think you could forgive your family member? Jesus' model prayer in Matthew 6:9–13, often called the Lord's Prayer, warns about forgiving others: "Our Father . . . forgive us our debts [or trespasses], as we also have forgiven our debtors." What if God forgave you only when you had forgiven others? He says, "You have burdened me with your sins and wearied me with your offenses. [Yet] I, even I, am he who blots out your transgressions, for my own sake, and remembers your sins no more" (Isaiah 43:24–25). Because of who He is, God's nature is merciful and forgiving. Not only that, He claims you as His child. You're in the perfect family, the family of God!

You may have to suffer humility to forgive someone, but isn't the reward worth it? Can you set aside your pride and open up your heart to a family member who's not where he or she should be in relationship with you? Even if you're weary trying to mend the relationship, can you, like God, who is burdened with *your* sins and wearied by *your* offenses, "remember their sins no more"? When I think of His sacrifice, giving His own Son, Jesus, for me, I know that I have a long way to go in my ability to forgive.

Do you need to forgive a family member?

Why or why not?

Share with your study friend, as you feel comfortable.

Remember Sin No More

Now look again at the last part of Hebrews 2:13: "Here am I, and the children God has given me." Christian quotes Isaiah 8:18 to assure you that you're safe in God's hands. Jesus, the Good Shepherd, says about us, His sheep, "My Father, who has given them to me, is greater than all; no one can snatch them out of my Father's hand. I and the Father are one" (John 10:29). You don't need to fear humiliation, harm, or even death! As an adopted sister of Christ Himself, you can have confidence in Christ!

My brother, whom I loved dearly, died three years ago, and I have missed him greatly. We had "inside jokes" no one else understood. I treasure my sister, Phyllis, more than ever. A great joy in my life, she and her immediate family—Ken, Brant, Jenks, Kerington, Chad, Amber, and Kensley— are a wonderful addition to my own. We celebrate weddings, anniversaries, birthdays, and new babies like one big happy family! I have statewide calling so I can phone her anytime and talk as long as I like. If this is just a fore-taste of glory divine, can you imagine the celebrations we're going to have in heaven with the whole family of God?

✽ FRIEND TO FRIEND ✽

What difference does it make to you that Jesus claims you as family?

How is your own father like God, "Abba, Father"?

How is he different?

Touch My Heart, Lord Jesus

O, Jesus, You are the great I AM. Thank You for making me holy, because You are holy. Thank You for accepting me as a joint-heir with You, Dear Holy Brother. May I sing Your praises in every congregation! Help me to forgive others, in grateful appreciation for Your forgiveness. I'm glad I'm a part of the family of God! Amen.

STUDY 5 *Lord, Help Me When I'm Afraid*
HEBREWS 2:14-18

FOR FOUR STUDIES you've focused on Jesus, your shining example. In this last study in the unit, you approach one of the most important subjects for all of us: fear. Everyone fears. Some of us refuse to admit it, but most of us have some kind of phobia: fear of the dark, the unknown, great heights, new experiences, or animals like spiders, bugs, large dogs, or bulls.

Fear causes us to do strange things. One summer, at age eight, I spent a week with my cousin Jane. Her mother made us each a shirt out of one yard of material, and we were amazed as we watched her cut out cloth and sew the pieces together. When we weren't being measured or trying on the work in progress, we played outside. One day Jane decided to climb a tree in the backyard. She sat on a limb, urging me to climb up beside her. The limb looked too high; it was over my head, for goodness' sake! I tried several times, swinging from the limb like a monkey and running my feet up the tree trunk to get high enough to latch on to the limb. I also tried jumping. Nothing worked. Each time, my hands would give out, or I'd scrape my leg; I had to drop to the ground before my feet caught the limb.

Then a large dog bounced around the corner of the house. When he saw me on the ground, he snarled, lunging at me. I don't remember the next few seconds, but I was instantly sitting on the limb with Jane!

"How'd you do that?" she asked.

"I don't know," I responded. "I just did it!"

Fear is a powerful motive for action! I can testify to that!

Things That Go Bump in the Night

Some people fear spiders. One of my high school friends could not even pronounce the word *spider*. She often told of her encounters with "SPs." One family member was caught in a culvert as a child while trying to retrieve a ball. Consequently, she has claustrophobia—fear of closed places, like elevators or caves. People who fear life commit suicide. People who fear death shrink away from life.

If you fear death, that fear can hold you as a slave. Unspoken, it can loom large in your mind and overcome your sense of confidence and trust in God. Most of us can express our fears, and then they seem less frightening. I'm still scared of big dogs, but I have learned to laugh about it and to hold my hand out, open-palmed, in the face of strange dogs I meet. How about you? Do you have any fears?

Name some childhood fears:

Share with your study friend . . .

(1) a fear you have conquered

(2) a fear you have not yet overcome

How do you think God can help you calm your fears?

Experts tell us it's unlikely our fears will come true. Most things we fear will never happen. My "SP" friend has never been bitten by a spider. I have never been killed by a dog. No burglar has ever broken into my home, though I am afraid of strange noises that go bump in the night. (I blame that on murder mysteries and television.)

In Study 4 we ended with Jesus' words: "Here am I, and the children God has given me." Today we explore His relationship with us, the children of God. This study is about you, as you relate to Jesus. Read the following verses carefully and circle the words you think are startling or important.

> "Since the children have flesh and blood, he too shared in their
> humanity so that by his death he might destroy him who holds the
> power of death—that is, the devil—and free those who all their lives
> were held in slavery by their fear of death."—Hebrews 2:14–15

~ FRIEND TO FRIEND ~

In Hebrews 2:14–15, what are the two reasons Jesus shared in our humanity? So that by His death He might:

1.

2.

Share the words your circled with your study friend.

Jesus shared in our humanity and died for us for two reasons: (1) to destroy the devil, and (2) to free all of us who are held in slavery by fear of death.

Have you ever contemplated that your children and/or parents, your extended family, friends, and even you will die someday? It's amazing to me how many widows are so overcome by grief that they can't function. When I ask, "Didn't you know your husband was going to die some day?" they answer, "No. I never considered it." Death is a part of life, and it's a delusion to avoid it. It's the other side of the coin of life. For as long as I can remember, I've never feared death. For a Christian, this fear indicates lack of trust that God knows what He's doing—He's in control. You can trust Him absolutely.

Even before we married in 1957, my husband and I discussed what would happen if either of us died. We talked about where we were going (heaven) and how happy we were to say, like Paul, "as always Christ will be exalted in my body, whether by life or by death. For to me, to live is Christ and to die is gain" (Philippians 1:20–21). I knew I was headed for heaven. So did my husband. Mentally and emotionally we were ready. Facing that fear of death years ahead of time made the loss much easier when he died suddenly in 1980.

Some fear is good. Fear of burning keeps us from getting too close to a fire. Soloists say that "butterflies in the stomach" before a solo gives them an edge, keeping their musical notes from going flat. Even fear of death causes us to confront it and face Jesus as the Savior from all death and fear. But if you still feel enslaved by the idea of death (if it scares you to death!), then you are acting as if Jesus died in vain. He died to free you from the fear of death which holds you in slavery.

In the next verse (Hebrews 2:16), Christian tells how to overcome fear of death and gives us a reason to trust in Christ: "For surely it is not angels he helps, but Abraham's descendants." Who are Abraham's descendants? Yep, you guessed it. Abraham's descendants are those who believe (Galatians 3:7, 9). What a promise God gives you through these words! God doesn't focus on helping angels! He helps you!

☙ FRIEND TO FRIEND ☙

Have you ever been afraid of death?

Yes   No

Reasons to fear death:

Better reasons not to fear death:

Help Is on the Way

Listen as God speaks to you through Hebrews 2:17: "For this reason he had to be made like his brothers in every way, in order that he might become a merciful and faithful high priest in service to God, and that he might make atonement for the sins of the people."

Jesus is like His brothers and sisters—all of us in the family of God— that is, Christians, people who have a relationship with Him. The next verse (Hebrews 2:18) identifies another way He is like us: "Because he him- self suffered when he was tempted, he is able to help those who are being tempted." He's been there! The key word in this sentence is "able." Jesus is able! He is capable of taking all your fear away. As our high priest, He has all authority from God!

❧ FRIEND TO FRIEND ❧

Reasons to talk about the hope I have in heaven ahead of time, before I go there:

Share your answers with your study friend.

In Hebrews 2:17–18, identify two character traits of Jesus, our High Priest.

1.

2.

As our High Priest, what does He do?

How do you know He understands your suffering when you are tempted to do wrong?

Share with your study friend.

Touch My Heart, Lord Jesus

Thank You, God, for sending Jesus, Your merciful, faithful Son. When I suffer pain, help me rejoice that He understands because He has experienced it like all humans. Thank You for making Him totally human, subject to temptation, and yet totally divine, never sinning. When I'm afraid, help me remember I can trust Him because He is able! Amen.

UNIT 2 *Jesus, Lord of All, My Lord*

GODLY WOMAN, holy sister, you have faced Jesus, your shining example, in Unit I. Now it's time to deepen that relationship by fixing your eyes on Him, to look for the Way! As you study the next segment of Hebrews, lean your ear toward Him, and listen to His voice. Placing your hand in His, hold firmly till the end. Trusting your home to Him, serve Him with all your heart.

In this unit you'll learn how to worship Jesus Christ, Lord of all—your High Priest, the Lord of history, and Savior of grace. If you're tired, you can learn how to rest in Him. If you need energy and power, you can learn how to be a faith professor—who professes her faith in Jesus, with confidence in Him. As you study, you may uncover the truth in one study and then dress in righteousness in the next. Can't wait to begin? Go!

STUDY 6 *God's House, My Home*
HEBREWS 3:1–6

Hebrews 3
My brothers, with salvation won,
Who share with me the heavenly call,
Just fix your thoughts on Him . . . the Son!
The Worthy One, our All in all.

Hold to your courage, faithful best!
For Jesus, greatest of them all—
Above great Moses and the rest,
Will issue you the final call.

Today then, if you hear His voice,
Hold not a turning, sinful heart.
With eyes on Him, your hurt to hoist,
To throw away, and then to part.
Encourage brothers, sisters, too:
Now, live! Hold firmly till the end!
You *can* approach the living God
And touch Him, friend to Friend!

—EDNA M. ELLISON, © 2002

I have built only one house in my lifetime, but I would not want to do it again! One day when our new house was being built, a neighbor, Dawn Sease, called.

"Edna, your house is on fire."

"Oh! I need to run out!" I grabbed the baby and glanced around frantically, but saw no fire. "Can you see it on the roof?"

"No. Don't run outside! It's your new house, not the one you live in now!"

I rushed out of the house with a wide-eyed baby who had never seen me jerk him up so fast and drove to the new house. On the new lawn stood two fire trucks and a host of firemen and neighbors. The firemen had extinguished the blaze by the time we got there, but our new home was damaged. On this cold day, workmen had lit a kerosene heater in the family room, and one of them had stumbled over it, spilling kerosene, which quickly caught on fire and spread into the attic. These workmen were careless builders. As we negotiated repair costs and a new price on the now-damaged house, the contractor, said, "Well, we're all human; these boys just made a little mistake."

In this study, let's consider the Perfect Builder, Jesus Christ: "Therefore, holy brothers [or sisters], who share in the heavenly calling, fix your thoughts on Jesus, the apostle and high priest whom we confess" (Hebrews 3:1). Hallelujah! He is not a careless builder. He makes no mistakes (Hebrews 3:1–6).

⁓ FRIEND TO FRIEND ⁓

What habits have you cultivated to help you focus, or fix, your thoughts on Jesus that make your quiet time with Him more meaningful?

How can you and your study friend fix your thoughts on Jesus now?

Share your ideas and pray.

The first words in Hebrews 3 refer to you, holy sister. What do those words mean to you? I think I'm pretty *holey*, with a bunch of holes in my armor, but I resist the word without the *e—holy*. God has convicted me that this feeling of false humility is the most popular trick of Satan, to make Christians feel unworthy of holiness. Will you enter with me in a period of soul searching right now?

OK. What makes you holy? Good works? No. Service in your church or denomination? No. Missions trips to the other side of the world? No. Great sacrifice for God? No.

What makes you holy is Jesus. When He enters your heart, His presence brings righteousness. His *at-one-ment* (*atonement*), or sacrifice on the Cross, made you *at one* with God, as Christ became the bridge of righteousness that brought you into right relationship with your Creator. You, godly woman, are a saint, holy in the eyes of God, if you have been saved from your sins, by Jesus, who died in your place.

If you refuse to admit you are a godly woman (and many Christian women do), then who do you think will be Christ's witness in the world? You may be the only one He has to share Him in your community. You're it. That's why He chose to make you holy, to be His representative in your area of influence, right where you are.

Share in the Heavenly Calling

Look back at Hebrews 3:1. The last half of the verse refers to Jesus, who is called (1) apostle and (2) high priest, whom we confess. How long has it been since you've confessed Jesus is the apostle and high priest? All right, I know I've no right to ask you that question until I've done it. I admit that I've never used those words when confessing Jesus. I'm vowing now to acknowledge Him as each of these.

The word *apostle* comes from the Greek word *apostolos*, meaning "I send." Paul says he is an apostle commissioned by Christ as a missionary (Romans 1:1; Galatians 1:1), and he also points to Jesus' brother James as an apostle (Galatians 1:19). Revelation 21:14 describes the walls of heaven as having 12 foundations, each listing one of the 12 apostles of the Lamb, who are Jesus' first disciples (Matthias replacing Judas Iscariot—Acts 1:15–26).

In future studies we shall also discuss how Jesus is our high priest (mediator, or bridge to God), as well as the superior apostle, the "One sent" from heaven!

⊷ FRIEND TO FRIEND ⊷

Spend time with your study friend brainstorming a list of characteristics of an apostle and a high priest.

Praise God that He has given Jesus these characteristics as an example to us.

Comparing Moses and Jesus

For centuries, Moses has been respected as a holy man by the Arab world and the Jewish world. Charlton Heston tells that when he was making the movie *The Ten Commandments*, thousands of Bedouin peasants whispered "Mo-sah" with downcast eyes as he walked among them, to show their respect for Moses.

In Hebrews 3:2, find the word that tells how Moses and Jesus were alike:

"He was faithful to the one who appointed him, just as Moses was faithful in all God's house."

The most important word to describe Jesus is *faithful*. Aren't you grateful you can depend on Him?

In the next verse, Hebrews 3:3, find the words that tell how Moses and Jesus were different:

"Jesus has been found worthy of greater honor than Moses, just as the builder of a house has greater honor than the house itself."

God Is the Builder; You're the House

The next verses explain why Jesus is worthy of greater honor than Moses: "For every house is built by someone, but God is the builder of everything. Moses was faithful as a servant in all God's house, testifying to what would be said in the future. But Christ is faithful as a son over God's house. And we are his house, if we hold on to our courage and the hope of which we boast" (Hebrews 3:4–6).

✢ FRIEND TO FRIEND ✢

Read Hebrews 3:4–6 and fill in the blanks below:

God is the _____ of _____.
Moses was faithful as a _____. Christ is faithful as a
_____ . We are God's _____.

Why do you think God inspired Christian to include these words comparing the servant in the house and the Son over the house?

Who owns the house?

Who owns your dwelling place?

Share with your study partner.

How did you fill in the blanks in the sidebar? Here's the way I filled them: God is the builder of everything. Moses was faithful as a servant. Christ is faithful as a son. We are God's house. God inspired these words in Hebrews to show us that Jesus, the Messiah, has fulfilled the Old Testament. Moses, the great hero, stands, as we all do, *insignificant* compared to our Redeemer and High Priest. God owns the house in Hebrews 3, just as He owns everything about you. Will you join me as I now acknowledge Him as the owner of my home and my heart?

For the last blank, you may have added this condition: we are God's house only *if* "we hold on to our courage and the hope of which we boast." The key words here are *hold on.* You're empowered to hold on with courage and hope when Jesus, the master builder, changes your heart and strengthens you, His building. He makes your timbers strong and braces you against the wind. Then you can endure with joy, regardless of circumstances! Because you have been built on a rock—the Rock of ages, Jesus Christ—as your cornerstone, you can withstand the storms of life (Matthew 7:24–27).

What would change in your life if you more fully submitted to Christ's rightful authority over you?

Share with your study friend how He is the builder of your life.

Touch My Heart, Lord Jesus
O, perfect builder of my heart, I bow before You today as my holy apostle and high priest. Thank You for giving me the heavenly lumber of courage and hope. O, faithful, living Son of God, may I be still before You, as Your house. Make the changes to my blueprints to suit Your plan. Come dwell here and build my heart. Amen.

STUDY 7 *God's Heart, My Ear*

SEVERAL YEARS AGO, this anonymous joke went all over the world by email: a man driving on a winding road met a woman driving the other way who shouted out her car window, "Pig!" He was outraged, thinking his recent weight gain couldn't possibly make him fat enough to be insulted in such a way. A moment later a large man in a blue convertible came around a bend and shouted, "Pig!" He shouted back, "You're a big hog yourself!"—just before he went around the curve and ran right into a large pig, wrecking his car.

Sometimes we just don't listen—to parents, to friends, to our consciences, or, most importantly, to God. At times we listen, but we're so bored with the gospel or so blinded by our own prejudice that we can't interpret the message. "So, as the Holy Spirit says: 'Today, if you hear his voice, do not harden your hearts as you did in the rebellion, during the time of testing in the desert, where your fathers tested and tried me and for forty years saw what I did'" (Hebrews 3:7–9).

◦✄ FRIEND TO FRIEND ✄◦

In Hebrews 3:7–9, who speaks?

What does He ask you not to do?

Do you remember a time when you hardened your heart as the Israelites did in their rebellious period in the Sinai desert? What happened?

The Hebrews writer, Christian, invites you to listen to the words of the Spirit of God, who speaks in a mysterious way, straight to your heart. You may hear almost a whisper of the Holy Spirit in your ear now. His message is simple: do not harden your heart. Remember this: God's redemption plan—His plan for you—is always to have relationship with you. He yearns to have you love Him. Much like us, the Hebrew fathers refused to listen to what God asked them to do, even though He had provided lavishly for them. He led them with a cloud during the day and a pillar of fire at night. He gave them heaven-bread, manna, and quail to eat, and provided water at appropriate times.

FRIENDSHIPS OF FAITH · 37

Even though God saved them from Pharaoh and parted the Red Sea (Exodus 15:19), they were rebellious from the beginning of their journey (Exodus 14:10–12). They refused to follow directions about the manna God had sent. Their greed caused them to hoard the manna (Exodus 16:19–20), but it spoiled. They even worshipped a golden calf they made while Moses was on Mt. Sinai receiving the Ten Commandments (Exodus 32:1–35)! [Extra reading: Exodus 15:19 to 16:30.]

However, if you know this story well, you're aware of a truth we still see today: God does not provide for our needs on our timetables, but in His perfect timing. One night as I was reading my Bible and fuming over an unanswered prayer, I said, "Lord, I want an answer and I want it now!"

Talk about hearing a whisper . . . I heard what seemed an audible voice as I read these words from Isaiah 49:8: "In the time of *my* favor I will answer you" (emphasis mine).

I remember scrambling quickly to apologize. "Lord, I'm sorry," I said. "I know better than that. I'm sorry I was impatient and rude. You are in charge. I'll wait until You let me know . . . just whenever You want to." Then I read Ecclesiastes 8:5: "The wise heart will know the proper time and procedure."

The Israelites rebelled against Moses, the leader God had chosen to take them away from slavery. God is not pleased when we think we are in charge. He says, "That is why I was angry with that generation, and I said, 'Their hearts are always going astray, and they have not known my ways.' So I declared an oath in my anger, 'They shall never enter my rest'" (Hebrews 3:10–11). These words, repeated from Psalm 95:7–11, tell the end of the sad story of the rebellious Israelites. They were not allowed to enter the rest of the promised land until 40 years later, when their generation had died out completely, so that a new generation of worshippers could turn sincerely to God.

❧ FRIEND TO FRIEND ❧

How did the Israelites test and try God? (See Exodus 15:22 to 16:30.)

In what ways did they see what God did? (See Exodus 15:19 to 16:18.)

Why do you think they had to stay in the wilderness for 40 years?

Hold On to the Wonder

What great advice Christian gives us in verse 12: "See to it, brothers, that none of you has a sinful, unbelieving heart that turns away from the living God."

Christian gives us ways to keep on track in our relationships with God and fellow Christians: "But encourage one another daily, as long as it is called Today, so that none of you may be hardened by sin's deceitfulness" (Hebrews 3:13). Don't waste one day. As you open your heart to allow Jesus to encourage you through prayer and Bible study, get out and encourage others. Don't let even one of your friends fall into Satan's deceitful trap of sin. As a dear friend, you have the privilege—every day—of encouraging. As you go about your daily tasks, you carry the Spirit of God with you.

❧ FRIEND TO FRIEND ❧

What are you doing to ensure that you do not have a sinful, unbelieving heart?

How do you avoid turning away from God and instead turning toward a relationship with Him?

Share with your study friend.

At a conference in Bakersfield, California, I once heard a pastor say, "O, Christian, hold on to the wonder . . . the wonder of your salvation." Remember how it was . . . keep thinking of it . . . don't ever forget His mercy. Do you remember when you first knew you were His? That He loved you, and that you could trust in Jesus alone for your salvation, that is, to usher you into heaven? Do you forget that moment in the hubbub of daily work? Don't forget! Direct your spirit to hold its awe of that moment. Think of it often. Hold on to the wonder!

Read Hebrews 3:13–14 carefully. Describe the confidence you had when you first became a Christian.

Did you think you'd become sinless and be the best person you could be? Did you believe you'd be a missionary?

Have you been disappointed since then that you could not be a perfect Christian?

What does it mean to be a perfect Christian?

What reward can you expect as you hold firmly, confident in Jesus?

Christian says, "We have come to share in Christ if we hold firmly till the end the confidence we had at first" (Hebrews 3:14). I'll never forget the night I became a Christian, just before I became a teenager. Mother had let my brother Jim and me go to bed dusty and dirty, without a bath, for the first time I could remember. Also for the first time, I heard God speak directly to me in my heart. Unable to sleep, I lay in gritty sheets contemplating words I had heard that morning at Vacation Bible School, awakening for the first time to His voice. I began to listen in a new way! I remember saying, "Lord Jesus, I am dirty inside and out; I've done a lot of mean things, and I'm sorry. I don't have any idea why an Almighty God would want to have a relationship with me. I have no knowledge, no power, no influence, no talent; but whatever I have, I give to You." What joy He brought into my heart! I still smile when I think of it. I want to remember that feeling—and way of thinking—forever.

Listen, Obey, Hold Firmly

Christian gives emphasis to his thoughts by repeating them: "As has just been said: 'Today, if you hear his voice, do not harden your hearts as you did in the rebellion.' Who were they who heard and rebelled? Were they not all those Moses led out of Egypt? And with whom was he angry for 40 years? Was it not with those who sinned, whose bodies fell in the desert? And to whom did God swear that they would never enter his rest if not to those who disobeyed? So we see that they were not able to enter, because of their unbelief" (Hebrews 3:15–19).

Touch My Heart, Lord Jesus

Speaker to my heart, may I listen carefully and follow Your words. Lord, forgive me for my unbelief and my rebellious behavior. Thank You, Righteous One, for coming into my heart, bringing me righteousness, making me right with God. I stand in awe of You; may I hold on to the wonder of Your love, rest in it every day, and share it with others. Amen.

STUDY 8 *God's Creation, a Sabbath Rest*

HEBREWS 4:1–11

Hebrews 4

Now we can count this promise sure:
To enter His eternal rest,
A sabbath for His people true,
The great "Today" that God knows best.

We read His Word from day to day
We know that it is Truth alive.
A two-edged sword that finds its way.
O, living, active gift, survive

Within our hearts; please penetrate!
We are laid bare before Your eyes.
And through Your Word, forgive us straight
Our angry attitudes and lies.

Friend, we can face the throne of grace,
And even we, in sin, are freed!
By Jesus' death, suff'ring disgrace,
He helps us in our time of need.

—EDNA M. ELLISON, © 2002

HAVE YOU EVER BEEN EXHAUSTED? I have, once or twice in my lifetime. When I was about 14, my parents bought a new car. Although it rained the next Saturday, my dad decided to take us for a long ride in the new car. We rode on major highways, secondary roads, city streets, and finally on dirt roads in the country. And then the worst happened. Chugging up a long hill, the car began to slide. The wheels spun around but would not pull up the hill. We panicked when the rear of the car began to slide toward a large ravine on the right. "Everybody out!" my father said in an Archie Bunker tone. "Out!"

We piled out of the car, immediately sinking into deep mud. Of course, we three children rebelled and complained about how muddy our shoes and clothes were.

"Everybody push!"

Mother nodded to us, and we stepped behind the rear tire, which spun mud like a lettuce spinner spewing out water. I was soaked and chilled to the bone.

"Harder!" Daddy shouted several times, from the drivers' seat. The car didn't move. Mother suggested we let Jim, who after all was nearly grown at age 13, steer the car until we got to the top of the hill. Daddy agreed. They swapped positions, with Jim stepping in to muddy the floor around the driver's seat and Daddy giving the old heave-ho to the back bumper. The car still did not move. Gratefully we stopped pushing to plan a strategy.

Daddy spotted burlap bags hanging on a fence near a hog wallow nearby. He climbed through, with me helping to grab the burlap bags, afraid we'd be arrested at any moment for theft. With his help, my sister—four-year-old Phyllis—and Mother and I put the bags under the tire for traction. When one bag sank, we'd place another one under the tire, with each tire gripping and then slipping. An hour later, the car had steadied itself in the middle of the road, and we crept up the hill to a paved road.

I'll never forget the welcomed rest at the top of the hill, as we flopped in, coloring the inside of the new car with red-brown mud to match the outside! All of us went to bed early that night,

Entering a Sweet Rest

Christian, our name for the writer of Hebrews, says, "Therefore, since the promise of entering his rest still stands, let us be careful that none of you be found to have fallen short of it" (Hebrews 4:1). He reminds the Hebrews (to whom he wrote this letter) that their ancestors—the Israelites, who left Egypt to find the promised land—had failed to enter God's rest: "For we also have had the gospel preached to us, just as they did; but the message they heard was of no value to them, because those who heard did not combine it with faith. Now we who have believed enter that rest, just as God has said, 'So I declared on oath in my anger, "They shall never enter my rest"'" (Hebrews 4:2–3).

The next sentences clarify what God's rest is: "And yet his work has been finished since the creation of the world. For somewhere he has spoken about the seventh day in these words: 'And on the seventh day God rested from all his work'" (Hebrews 4:3–4).

The "somewhere" mentioned in verse 4 is in Genesis: "By the seventh day God had finished the work he had been doing; so on the seventh day he rested from all his work. And God blessed the seventh day and made it holy, because on it he rested from all the work of creating that he had done" (Genesis 2:2–3).

Christian explains the previous verses, comparing two ways of approaching the rest: "And again in the passage above he says, 'They shall never enter my rest.' It still remains that some will enter that rest, and those who formerly had the gospel preached to them did not go in, because of their disobedience" (Hebrews 4:5–6). [For extra reading, see Joshua 1:13; 11:23.]

✄ FRIEND TO FRIEND ✄

Of the choices below, which do you prefer?

a) Doing things my way, not cowing down to any authority. Who cares about rest? I'm high energy!

b) Being obedient, becoming a servant, and entering the rest at some future time. I have patience.

c) I don't know yet; I'm confused about why God would not love the Israelites enough to let them enter the promised land and rest regardless of what they'd done.

d) I believe God let some of them enter His rest, even though He may have promised not to.

Share ideas with your study friend.

Today's the Day

God is a just God, and He keeps His promises, whether they are a blessing or a warning. He had given His rebellious people a warning, and, because of His faithful nature, He has to uphold His word. However, God's overwhelming blessing is His great love for us. Christian speaks of His mercy and love: "Therefore, God again set a certain day, calling it Today, when a long time later he spoke through David, as was said before: 'Today, if you hear his voice, do not harden your hearts'" (Hebrews 4:7).

I love reading in Hebrews because of Christian's logical style. Here are his steps.

1. We know that God is just.

2. We also know He is love.

3. We know He must punish rebellion and sin.

4. We know the Israelites sinned. (They complained, refused to trust God, and proved themselves cowards in the face of the Egyptians and the Canaanites in the promised land. They refused to follow Moses, complaining and whining, hoarding the manna God provided, and even worshipping idols like the golden calf.)

5. We know God promised under oath they would not receive His rest in the promised land because of their disobedience.

6. We know God held to His promise; none of that disobedient generation entered the promised land. Yet God's representatives—Moses and his assistant, Joshua—kept God's law and God's oath alive. (We know they did because later God spoke to David, giving his people another chance at redemption.)

Christian says, "For if Joshua had given them rest, God would not have spoken later about another day" (Hebrews 4:8). He concludes this logical treatise with these words: "There remains, then, a Sabbath-rest for the people of God; for anyone who enters God's rest also rests from his own work, just as God did from his" (Hebrews 4:9–10).

Christian reader, have you claimed that Sabbath-rest? God's rest is the best rest. He provides it for us. He knows our physical, mental, emotional, social, and spiritual need for rest. Think about each of these areas of your life, and decide ways you can go to God for that rest.

Physical (nutrition/food, drink, sleep, exercise, weight, medical/dental checkups, or other physical stress):

Mental (educational study, work reports, church study, tutoring others, children's homework, computer information/choices, or other mental-stress issues):

Emotional (worry, problems with family/co-workers, manipulating/

being manipulated, hormonal considerations, fear, self worth, or other emotional-stress issues):

Social (entertaining, friendships, parties, watching TV, games, healthful activities with others, choices, or other social-stress issues):

Spiritual (trusting God, patience, resting on His Word, Bible study, meditation, praise, singing, faith, joy in Christ, self worth, or other spiritual-stress issues):

⊰ FRIEND TO FRIEND ⊱

Share with your study partner what kind of rest you feel you need in each of these areas.

Christian ends the passage with this invitation: "Let us, therefore, make every effort to enter that rest, so that no one will fall by following their example of disobedience" (Hebrews 4:11). Who is "their" in this verse? The disobedient Israelites who did not enter the promised land, where they would have found a home of rest.

God still issues that invitation to us today. Today!

We can still find a home, a resting place with Jesus. About 2,000 ago, Jesus said, "Come unto me, all ye that labor and are heavy laden, and I will give you rest" (Matthew 11:28 KJV). If you need rest, remember, God's Word includes the story of the Israelites' failure as an example for you and me today. We can still take advantage of the invitation to rest.

Touch My Heart, Lord Jesus
O, Lord of the Sabbath, thank You for Your promise of eternal rest with You. Forgive me when I, like the Israelites, get so caught up in the busyness of today's culture that I forget Whose I am. I depend on Your rest, O, God. Refresh me this day; lead me in the way of complete Sabbath rest according to Your Word. Amen.

STUDY 9 *God's Word, a Two-Edged Sword*

HEBREWS 4:12–13

ONE WINTER our family had experienced many illnesses—without health insurance. Jack, then four, had a tricycle mishap and went to the hospital with a concussion. The baby, Patsy, had been in and out of the doctor's office with allergies, asthma, and bronchitis. We were glad to see the winter end, with sunny days on the horizon. In those days tax season came in March. (The ides of March, March 15, was notorious.) We spent January and February eating the cheapest cuts of meat and denying ourselves any entertainment or treats so we could pay the city, county, state, and federal taxes on that big deadline day. Late on Friday, March 14, we finally scraped up the money, and my husband mailed off the IRS and state checks, stopping by city hall and then driving to the county auditor's office to deliver our hard-earned money. When he returned home, he found to his surprise that he had the county receipt stamped "paid" tucked behind our uncashed check (the largest of the three he'd written).

He blinked. "What do you make of this?" he asked.

"The receipt and our check back . . . hmm . . . I think God is blessing us with dollars to replace the ones we've spent this winter," I said. "We'll keep it, of course. We have the receipt, for goodness' sake! We'd be stupid to try to pay it twice." I'm ashamed of myself now, but it sounded like a good plan at the time.

"We can't keep it," he said firmly. "I'll return it Monday."

"Let's pray about it. Maybe God does intend for us to keep it." That weekend I did pray; I prayed that my husband would change his mind. I had sacrificed too long. We deserved a little cash back to spend, and besides, who would know? All day Saturday we talked about why we should return the check, to be honest citizens. All day I kept hoping for a lightning bolt from God or handwriting on the wall saying, "Keep the money, kids. You deserve this special gift from Me. Love, God."

I went to church Sunday morning certain that God was rewarding us. Then in an opening devotional, I heard, "Render unto Caesar what is Caesar's, and unto God what is God's." God's Word became a sharp sword that cut straight to my heart. How could I have been so blinded by greed that I thought cheating my government was right? I accompanied my husband the next day, and we celebrated with an ice-cream sundae after we returned the money! We made the clerk happy; she had to pay the money in her shortfall. She thanked us again and again for being honest. (I knew my husband was staunchly honest, but it took words from the Bible to put me straight and right with God.)

❧ FRIEND TO FRIEND ❧

Have you ever been tempted to be dishonest? What happened?

Has God's Word ever convicted you of wrongdoing? What happened?

Share with your study friend what you learned from these experiences.

As a child, I sang this song: "I stand alone on the Word of God, the B-I-B-L-E!" Today's study will concentrate on the power of God's Word. Read below the words from a few of my favorite Scripture verses. Open your heart as you slowly read each word. As God teaches you, circle in each passage the most important word(s) you feel He is emphasizing:

2 PETER 3:5—"By God's word the heavens existed and the earth was formed."

ACTS 10:36—"The message [word] God sent."

JOHN 17:17—"Your word is truth."

JOHN 1:1—"The Word was God . . . [and] was with God in the beginning."

JOHN 5:24—"Whoever hears my word and believes . . . has eternal life."

MATTHEW 13:22—"Worries . . . and the deceitfulness of wealth choke it [the word]."

2 CORINTHIANS 5:19—"He has committed to us the message [word] of reconciliation."

PHILIPPIANS 1:14—"Because of my chains . . . [others] speak the word of God more courageously."

2 TIMOTHY 2:9—"God's word is not chained."

PSALM 119:105 — "Your word is a lamp to my feet and a light for my path."

JAMES 1:22 — "Do not merely listen to the word. . . . Do what it says."

1 PETER 1:25 — "The word of the Lord stands forever."

ᕱ FRIEND TO FRIEND ᕱ

Discuss with your study friend the most significant words you circled in the passages about God's Word.

Which of the Scriptures applies to Edna's story of returning the tax money?

ᕱ FRIEND TO FRIEND ᕱ

Christian, our name for the writer of Hebrews, says, "For the word of God is living and active. Sharper than any double-edged sword, it penetrates even to dividing soul and spirit, joints and marrow; it judges the thoughts and attitudes of the heart" (Hebrews 4:12). How often have you doubted God or had mean or unfaithful thoughts, yet God led you back to faithfulness through an unexpected brush with His Word? Matthew 13:22 lists worries and greed as two things that choke the Word, that blind us to words of truth. Like the story at the beginning of this study, has someone quoted a Scripture verse that led you back to Him? Maybe you saw a sign that reminded you of God's truth, or you heard a Christian speaker, almost by accident, as you surfed channels—all these were no mere coincidences. God's Word definitely has power to be at the right place at the right time, to penetrate our hearts. "All Scripture is God-breathed and is useful for teaching, rebuking, correcting and training in righteousness, so that the man of God may be thoroughly equipped for every good work" (2 Timothy 3:16–17).

Read Hebrews 4:12 again; what does the Word of God judge? When you open your Bible, you open your heart to dynamic, living words that cut to the heart, causing you to face yourself and your sin. God judges not only your actions but also your thoughts and the attitudes of your heart. Scriptures are double-edged because they seem to be one thing on the surface, but have a supernatural side even more powerful than the side we see at first, on the pages of our Bibles. We are concerned with the earthly; God is concerned with the heavenly. Our words speak of earthly ideas; His Word speaks of heavenly ideas.

Paul says, "Since, then, you have been raised with Christ, set your hearts on things above, where Christ is seated at the right hand of God" (Colossians 3:1). Try this "heavenly" experiment: read the following words from Colossians 3 and see where God stops you. Pray as you read, asking Him to help you pause on words that will teach you something personal. Record your thoughts in the sidebar.

"Put to death, therefore, whatever belongs to your earthly nature: sexual immorality, impurity, lust, evil desires and greed, which is idolatry. Because of these, the wrath of God is coming. You used to walk in these ways, in the life you once lived. But now you must rid yourselves of all such things as these: anger, rage, malice, slander, and filthy language from your lips. Do not lie to each other, since you have taken off your old self with its practices and have put on the new self, which is being renewed in knowledge in the image of its Creator."

—Colossians 3:5–10

"As God's chosen people, holy and dearly loved, clothe yourselves with compassion, kindness, humility, gentleness and patience. Bear with each other and forgive whatever grievances you may have against one another. Forgive as the Lord forgave you. And over all these virtues put on love, which binds them all together in perfect unity."

—Colossians 3:12–14

✿ FRIEND TO FRIEND ✿

Write what God teaches you from Colossians 3.

Share with your study friend at least one truth God has shown you and what you plan to do about it.

Lord, You Uncover the Covered Truth
As I related in Study 8, the night I became a Christian, I became aware of my dirt—my sin—and aware of God's Spirit, who established relationship

with me in a personal way that night. It has been the most exciting relationship of my life!

Christian points out that God sees your motives as well as your actions. As you read God's Word, He convicts you of inner sin (dirty heart) as well as outer sin (dirty actions). His Word uncovers your sin and reveals it, bringing mercy and peace to your heart. "Nothing in all creation is hidden from God's sight. Everything is uncovered and laid bare before the eyes of him to whom we must give account" (Hebrews 4:13).

Touch My Heart, Lord Jesus

Help me find Your message in Your holy Word, O God. I willingly open my soul to You. I now uncover everything in my heart and soul and lay them bare before You. Judge my thoughts and attitudes and show me what I need to coincide with Your will. I love You, Lord; I know You'll lead me as I move closer to You, studying Your Word. Amen.

❧ FRIEND TO FRIEND ❧

STUDY 10 *God's High Priest, a Savior of Grace*
HEBREWS 4:14–16

JAN HIGH, a friend from North Carolina, told me this story about emeritus missionary Caroline Jones's daughter, Libby. After Libby had an outburst one day, Caroline had sent four-year-old Libby to her room for time-out. Later when Caroline checked on her, she found Libby with hands folded, praying, "O, Mickey Mouse, if only you were here, you'd know what to do. O, Mickey . . ." Because of her Christian parents, Libby had seen a model for praying, but hadn't quite learned to pray to the right person. Mickey Mouse was not the source for Libby's power to overcome problems. With her parents' guidance, she would soon learn to pray to the One with the power, Jesus Christ, in whom she could have faith and trust. Then she learned how to grow to adulthood managing her anger and her behavior, as all of us must do.

We finish this unit on "Jesus, Lord of All" by looking at what Christian, our name for the writer of Hebrews, says about our faith in Christ: "Therefore, since we have a great high priest who has gone through the heavens, Jesus the Son of God, let us hold firmly to the faith we profess" (Hebrews 4:14). This verse has two parts: (1) a description of Jesus and (2) a command for us. Before you read further, let's identify these.

❧ FRIEND TO FRIEND ❧

Using Hebrews 4:14, fill in the blanks below. Description of Jesus:

Jesus is a _____ who has gone
_____and is the _____
of _____. Command for us: Let us _____
_____ to the _____
we _____.

So, I'm a Faith Professor

For logical order of action, begin with the command. What does it mean to "hold firmly"? Isaiah 7:9 emphasizes the importance of holding firm: "If you do not stand firm in your faith, you will not stand at all."

OK. You get it. You are to grasp tenaciously—hold on with all you've got—the faith in Jesus that you profess. What does *profess* mean? Like most *professors*, you can teach only from the overflow of your heart and mind. If you're passionate about your faith, you make an open avowal of it. You may call this your *profession of faith*, but it's not just one moment of public acceptance of Christ in your church. It's continuing action. You announce, yes; but you also declare, teach, and share it everywhere you go. You're a faith professor through hard times and good, through the best days of euphoric joy and the worst days of despair over life's puzzles you can't untangle. You stand on the promises of God daily, hourly, by the moment, and by each second. Actually, the process shouldn't be *continual* (stopping and starting) but *continuous* (uninterrupted, without break).

Look back at the first part of Hebrews 4:14, the description of Jesus: "Therefore, since we have a great high priest who has gone through the heavens, Jesus the Son of God." Christian calls Jesus three things: (1) a great high priest, (2) one who has gone through the heavens, and (3) the Son of God. In Study 11 we'll explore more fully the definition of *high priest*. Until then, be thinking of what a high priest does. What was a priest's function in the Old Testament? What is it today in postmodern denominations? belong to a denomination with no ministers called high priests, but according to friends and family who do, I know high priests are called by God, pray for people, are advocates for those in the church and community, and administer sacraments (or ordinances, such as baptism and communion) of the church.

Like Christian, I'm assured that Jesus went to heaven. Each Gospel (Matthew, Mark, Luke, and John) verifies His resurrection and ascension (see Luke 24). After He spoke to Mary Magdalene near the empty tomb,

He explained He had not yet gone to His Father in heaven (John 20:17), but Scriptures record that later He rose before the eyes of His disciples and others, lifted up to heaven in a dramatic ascension (Acts 1:9–11). The third characteristic in our description of Jesus brings this unit to a close. Jesus is the Son of God, a basic truth which we have discussed in previous chapters.

Notice the way Christian surrounds these three descriptors with words of encouragement: "Therefore, since we have [Jesus, described by these three characteristics] *let us* hold firmly." Christian, like you and me, is willing to encourage others by writing a letter to declare his own profession of faith and asks his fellow Christians to do the same. Paul writes the people in Thessalonica to encourage them: "So then, brothers, stand firm and hold to the teachings we passed on to you, whether by word of mouth or by letter" (2 Thessalonians 2:15).

How about you? Do you encourage others to hold firmly to their faith? In the face of cancer, depression, and death, do you profess your faith and passionately tell them you believe in the power of Jesus?

⊰ FRIEND TO FRIEND ⊱

In preparation for Study 11, interview several people, asking them for a definition of "high priest."

Discuss with your study friend what information/opinions you find.

Can you think of several people you know who would enjoy receiving a letter/emails from you encouraging them to hold firmly to their faith? Share your ideas with your study friend.

Pray together as you decide how many letters/ email to write and set a deadline for mailing.

The Great High Priest Is Able
Christian gives an extra qualification for Jesus, which makes Him superior to other high priests: "For we do not have a high priest who is unable to sympathize with our weaknesses, but we have one who has been tempted

in every way, just as we are—yet was without sin" (Hebrews 4:15). One of the most remarkable doctrines of Christianity—one that separates our religion from all others—is the Incarnate Christ; that is, that Jesus is 100 percent divine. He is totally God. At the same time, He became 100 percent human. The incarnate Jesus is totally a man. But He is God come down—the Word on earth.

Here's the explanation for the paradox of Jesus as fully God and fully human. When He left heaven to become a human being, He faced sin in every way we do, except that He did not succumb to it. Tested, tried, and tempted, He remained the Holy Messiah, the sinless Christ. As the incarnate (become carnal, or fleshly) Jesus, He is able to sympathize with our weaknesses. He became weak—like us—to face temptation as we do and bring death to sin's punishment forever.

What a Savior! What a sympathetic God who understands! Isn't it a comfort for you to know that Jesus understands? He understands how strong temptation is; He understands your heartache when you fail in purity of relationship. He even understands when you willingly sin and then repent and regret your failure. He forgives your sins, no matter how great they are.

Approach the King's Throne with Confidence

Christian explains the comfort we find in Jesus and the ease with which we can approach Him: "Let us then approach the throne of grace with confidence, so that we may receive mercy and find grace to help us in our time of need" (Hebrews 4:16). The throne is often called the "mercy seat." Made of pure gold, it was the top of the ark of the covenant. In the Old Testament, the presence of God rested on the mercy seat. It is still at Jesus' throne that we receive mercy and grace from Him, the Lamb, who sits today on the throne in heaven, according to Revelation.

❧ FRIEND TO FRIEND ❧

Fill in the blanks based on Hebrews 4:16.

Let us then _____the throne
of_____ with _____, so that we
may receive _____ and find _____ to
_____ us in our time of _____.

Share with your study friend.

Mercy means *not* getting the punishment we deserve. *Grace* means getting what we *don't* deserve: *God's Riches At Christ's Expense.* Jesus died for your sins and gave you the gift of eternal life, absolutely free. "May our Lord Jesus Christ himself and God our Father, who loved us and by his grace gave us eternal encouragement and good hope, encourage your hearts and strengthen you in every good deed and word" (2 Thessalonians 2:16–17). Because He was the incarnate Christ, living here as a man, yet divine, He can understand and encourage you. When you approach Him in heaven, you will have the home field advantage. Your High Priest is also your coach! He has paved the way for you to play there, to go to heaven, your real home.

God Answers Kneemail

How do you approach the throne? On your knees? Sure. It's true that God answers kneemail. He seeks your prayers and communication in a relationship with Him—but you can approach Him with confidence, as Christian says in Hebrews 4:16. (We'll discover more about this confidence in later studies.) He offers you three things: mercy, grace, and help in time of need. The best part is that He gives all of these things free. It costs Him everything, but He gives it freely to you because He loves you.

Touch My Heart, Lord Jesus

God of mercy and grace, how thankful I am that You love me. Help me, as my great High Priest, to encourage others as a "faith-professor," declaring Your love to them. May I always hold firmly to my faith in You, and approach Your throne with the confidence that only a believer can possess! Thank You, Lord of all, for being my Lord! Amen.

UNIT 3
Listening to God's Call

GODLY WOMAN, faith professor, listen to Him as you approach this unit. It will build on the Unit 1 study of Jesus as your shining example and the Unit 2 study of Jesus as Lord. In Unit 3, we will hear how God issues you a call to service, a call to maturity, a call to faithfulness, and a call to His promises. The most important theme of this unit is the comparison of the Old Testament priests to Jesus, our high priest. You will see Him as the better priest, the better sacrifice, and the One who offers the better promise, eternal life in heaven. You'll go behind the veil and see the most holy place, a foreshadowing of heaven. Christian will urge you to understand the foundational truths of the gospel and grow beyond the elementary things to live a mature life in God.

The unit ends with a focus on Jesus, the One who calls you. I know you're as eager to learn how to listen to Him as you would be to listen to an important person on the phone. Hear Him calling? Then let's begin, and listen to His call!

STUDY 11 *God's Call to Service*
HEBREWS 5:1–10

Hebrews 5
O Jesus, our High Priest on high
Who offers sacrifice for sin,
You gave Yourself, alone to die,
To give eternal life to men.

And like Melchizedek of old,
High priest with God, above the rest,
You stand alone as Savior, Lord,
Submissive One, God's very best.

Made perfect in Your body and soul
The glorified right hand of Him:
One who created all things whole
Though earthly sun will one day dim.

May we grow as we walk this sod,
To highest, elemental truths:
To seek the meat and fruit of God,
To grow in Him, in His pursuits.

—EDNA M. ELLISON, © 2002

IN STUDY 10 we explored the office of a high priest. In today's study, Christian, our name for the Hebrews writer, explains the nature of those priests. He says, "Every high priest is selected from among men and is appointed to represent them in matters related to God, to offer gifts and sacrifices for sins" (Hebrews 5:1). Let's dissect this verse.

Not just a few high priests, but *every* high priest is chosen in a special way: they're selected from among men. Now look at verse 4: "No one takes this honor upon himself; he must be called by God, just as Aaron was." When God called Moses from the burning bush (Exodus 3), He commanded Moses to tell Pharaoh to release the Israelites from slavery, allowing them to leave Egypt (Exodus 3:8–10). Moses gave several excuses, finally asking God to send someone else (Exodus 4:13). God then appointed Aaron, Moses' older brother (three years older—Exodus 7:7) as His spokesperson: "What about your brother, Aaron the Levite? I know he can speak well. . . . He will speak . . . and it will be as if he were your mouth" (Exodus 4:14, 16). Over and over Aaron commanded Pharaoh, "Let my people go" (Exodus 5:1). Aaron served as high priest, the people's advocate, the mediator between Pharaoh and the people of Israel.

Not everyone is called as a high priest, or clergy, but you (and every Christian) are called by God to serve Him. Peter tells his fellow Christians, "But you are a chosen people, a royal priesthood . . . that you may declare the praises of him who called you out of darkness into his wonderful light" (1 Peter 2:9). Some Christians call this the "priesthood of the believer"— that is, you can dare approach a holy God because you trust Jesus to be your high priest. You don't need an earthly go-between, like Aaron, or any mediator other than the Holy Spirit of the Lord, who intercedes for you. We'll learn more about Jesus as our high priest in further passages in Hebrews.

⚜ FRIEND TO FRIEND ⚜

How have you been selected from others and called by God?

Does God call just high priests or does He call everyone to a certain place of service?

What do you think the "priesthood of the believer" means?

Share with your study friend.

Dealing Gently with Ignorant People

Christian gives an additional task of an earthly high priest: "He is able to deal gently with those who are ignorant and are going astray, since he himself is subject to weakness. This is why he has to offer sacrifices for his own sins, as well as for the sins of the people" (Hebrews 5:2–3). Do you feel God has called *you* to deal gently with ignorant people? How does being "subject to weakness," or having a tendency to sin, qualify you to deal gently with others, perhaps forgiving them for *their* failures? What do you offer as a sacrifice for God?

❧ FRIEND TO FRIEND ❧

Circle the items below that you sacrifice to God:

My time

My talent

My home

My reading material

My possessions (money, car, clothes, other_____)

What other things do you sacrifice or dedicate to Him?

Share your ideas with your study friend.

Chosen by God

In Hebrews 5:4–5, Christian begins to compare the Old Testament high priest to Jesus the great high priest. We will continue the in-depth comparison of Old Testament priests to Jesus in the next few studies, culminating with Study 15. (If you want to read ahead, read Hebrews 7). Today's study will set the stage for that study. Look carefully at verse 4: "No one takes this honor upon himself; he must be called by God, just as Aaron was." God had to validate the priests' ministry by choosing them; they couldn't choose to become priests, setting up their own ministry. Verse 5 shows how Christ fulfilled this Scripture as a valid high priest: "So Christ also did not take upon himself the glory of becoming a high priest. But God said to him, 'You are my Son; today I have become your Father.' " Notice the honor God gave Jesus. Far above the ordinary high priest, he is the only Son of God the Father!

Christian quotes Psalm 110:4 in Hebrews 5:6: "And he says in another place, 'You are a priest forever, in the order of Melchizedek.' " The story of Melchizedek [Mell-KIHZ-eh-deck] comes from Genesis 14:18–20: "Then Melchizedek king of Salem brought out bread and wine. He was priest of God Most High, and he blessed Abram, saying, 'Blessed be Abram by God Most High, Creator of heaven and earth. And blessed be God Most High, who delivered your enemies into your hand.' Then Abram gave him a tenth of everything." Melchizedek lived early in the Hebrews' history, before they became a nation and before God gave them the Ten Commandments and other laws. He lived before the Israelites were slaves in Egypt and before God called Moses to lead them from Egypt to the promised land, to ordain priests to serve the people, and to order tithes to support them. We will find Melchizedek an interesting character as we study more about him in Hebrews.

Christian's words reflect the realization by the early Christians that Jesus was the Son of God who became our gateway to heaven. God honored Him, just as He had honored Melchizedek. He became your high priest, that is, your personal mediator as well as the sacrificial lamb offered for you. Jesus died in your place, just as the righteous Melchizedek and other righteous high priests offered lambs and other animals as sacrifices for their people.

In Hebrews 5:7–10, Christian compares Jesus to Melchizedek: "During the days of Jesus' life on earth, he offered up prayers and petitions with loud cries and tears to the one who could save him from death, and he was heard because of his reverent submission. Although he was a son, he learned obedience from what he suffered, and, once made perfect, he became the source of eternal salvation for all who obey him and was designated by God to be high priest in the order of Melchizedek."

Before His death on the Cross, Jesus said to His disciples: "My soul is overwhelmed with sorrow to the point of death." Then He prayed in the garden of Gethsemane: "My Father, if it is possible, may this cup be taken from me. Yet not as I will, but as you will." (Matthew 26:38–39). God was aware of Jesus' cries and tears as He prayed. Yet Jesus was, as Christian says, reverent in His submission to God's will. Although He was the only Son of God, He had learned obedience through His suffering in His life on earth, and once He died, becoming the lamb offered for our sin, He became the source of salvation.

Look back at Hebrews 5:7–10. For whom did Jesus become the source of salvation? Knowing the human pain He'd experience—and even begging not to have to suffer—He still laid down His life for *you*, opening your way to heaven. If you obey Him, then you can become an inheritor of eternal salvation. What great news!

Who do you believe was "the one who could save him" in Hebrews 5:7?

Does Hebrews 5:7–10 imply that Melchizedek was perfect?

How can you accept Jesus' perfect righteousness into your heart?

❧ Friend to Friend ❧

Why do you think God set examples of high priests in the Old Testament, including the prototype for high priests, Melchizedek?

How did Melchizedek serve as an example for the Israelites and fore-shadow the priesthood of Jesus, God's Son?

Share with your study partner.

Does Service Make Us Perfect?

Were the Levites or Melchizedek made perfect through their service or through their ordination? No. Just humans like us, these high priests were never perfect. Neither religious service (good works), nor ordination makes us perfect. However, because God loved us, He sacrificed His only Son, Jesus, the only one who was ever perfect, to bring us into right relationship with Himself. Though we who are imperfect don't deserve His mercy, we can accept into our hearts the indwelling Christ as our high priest, to make us right with the Almighty.

As Christian says, God also *saved* Jesus, who was resurrected from the dead! Because of His resurrection, we, too, have the hope of resurrection, as we follow Him in life and in the afterlife in heaven!

Touch My Heart, Lord Jesus

O Lamb of God, thank You for being obedient to God's redemption plan, opening the way to heaven for me. I can never thank You enough for dying for me on the Cross, in pain and suffering. How great Your love is! How far above me You are—high and lifted up! How far above even the great high priest, Melchizedek! I praise You, Lord, with a humble heart. Amen.

STUDY 12 *God's Call to Maturity*
HEBREWS 5:11-14

ONE OF MY FAVORITE PEOPLE at work used to say, "I've thought about so many things my head hurts! I'm wearing out my head from the inside out!" Did your head hurt after you finished Study 11? Mine did! We can learn deep truths from Hebrews 5:1–10. Christian, our name for the author of Hebrews, also found those verses difficult as he carefully chose words to explain Christianity to the Hebrews. Just think of it! Some of them were probably new Christians; the concepts of a new covenant, of Jesus as a new high priest, and a relationship with God, rather than just obedience to a set of laws, were difficult to understand. A giant paradigm shift had occurred, and they were living in a new world, under a new covenant with God!

Are you a new Christian, or have you been studying the Bible for a long time? You may feel comfortable studying doctrinal truths, or they may be difficult to grasp. Remember, God says, "I have much more to say to you, more than you can now bear. But when he, the Spirit of truth, comes, he will guide you into all truth" (John 16:12–13). I hope this Bible study of Hebrews has illuminated words or concepts you previously may not have understood.

⊰ FRIEND TO FRIEND ⊱

How long have you been a Christian?
In what kinds of Bible study have you participated?

How would you like to study about God in the future?

Share your ideas and understanding of God's Word with your study friend.

Ask your study friend to clarify terms or "churchy" words you do not understand, or look them up together in a Bible dictionary.

Following the deep truths about Melchizedek and Jesus as our new high priest, Christian pauses to say, "We have much to say about this, but it is hard to explain because you are slow to learn" (Hebrews 5:11). You can almost hear him say, "Whew! I'm getting a headache from talking about those Old Testament priests, Melchizedek and the Levites; history is important, but it's hard to explain. Maybe it's over your heads." Christian recognizes it's hard for his readers to learn new truths, foreign to their understanding, since they have a Jewish background and were probably trained to understand the Mosaic Law, not these new concepts.

Do you detect impatience in Christian's next words? "In fact, though by this time you ought to be teachers, you need someone to teach you the elementary truths of God's word all over again. You need milk, not solid food!" (Hebrews 5:12). Sometimes I feel as Christian does. Do you lose patience with people who don't get it? You watch family members or dear friends backslide, live in doubt, or abandon their faith from lack of use. You wonder why they failed to trust God with their lives. You may be tempted to say, "I give up! They'll never trust God or live a contented life." Or maybe you sometimes feel as if you are one of those people.

Using Hebrews 5:11–12, fill in the blanks below:

Christian describes the Hebrew Christians as slow to _____
(v. 11). He says: By this _____ you ought to be
_____. You need _____ to _____
you; you need _____, not _____ food (v. 12).

If he spoke those same words to you, how would you feel? Share these feelings with your study friend.

For 12 years I taught a Bible study every Sunday morning. Once, as we explored the Scriptures, a regular participant said, "I hope I'll go to heaven. Of course, nobody can be sure, but I hope I've been good enough." I was flabbergasted! We had discussed gospel truth hundreds of times, but she was dead wrong on two concepts: (1) she had to be good to get into heaven and (2) she couldn't depend on going there.

Explain how you plan to go to heaven.

What steps are you taking to get there?

Do you agree that being good (yourself; your own good deeds) is not the way to get there?

Do you think the goodness of Jesus is the way to get there? (The perfect [sinless] Lamb of God died as a sacrifice for you, and therefore—if you accept Him as your Savior—you will be seen as perfect when you are judged, and you will qualify for admittance into heaven.)

Is it difficult to believe that your good works do not count as an "entry ticket"?

❧ FRIEND TO FRIEND ❧

Share your thoughts with your study friend.

When that comment was made that Sunday, I stopped the regular study and we read Ephesians 2:8–9: "For it is by grace you have been saved, through faith—and this not from yourselves, it is the gift of God—not by works, so that no one can boast." We discussed how our own goodness does not save us (but Jesus' goodness does!). Then we studied John's words: "Jesus did many other miraculous signs in the presence of his disciples, which are not recorded in this book. But these are written that you may believe that Jesus is the Christ, the Son of God, and that by believing you may have life in his name" (John 20:30–31). "I write these things to you who believe in the name of the Son of God so that you may know that you have eternal life" (1 John 5:13). Any believer who wants to know may be sure she's going to heaven. God gave us the Bible so that you could *know for sure!*

That Sunday morning, when we finished our Bible study, our class member went out the door saying, "I've learned a little this morning. I'm still not sure, though. I still hope I'll be good enough to be in heaven!" Some of the class members shook their heads. How could she still not be sure? The Bible was written *so that she could be sure.* And *me.* And *you.* God wants you to be sure, absolutely positive, that you're going to heaven! I have no doubt I'll be there. Let's join each other there one day, in all the joy that comes from spending eternity with Jesus!

In defense of the Hebrew Christians, however, remember these folks were under tremendous stress. Because of persecution, they hid in caves (and the catacombs and sewers under Rome, among other places). They were fed to lions and other wild animals, crucified, beheaded, and served on platters. No wonder they were running scared!

Another factor was that they had few ministers/ missionaries to explain Jesus' sacrifice for them to have everlasting life without being slaves to Old Testament laws. The disciples scattered; many were killed. Missionaries like Paul (who persecuted Christians before he became one himself—much to his surprise!) could not visit the growing numbers of new Christians. They became itinerant preachers, traveling many miles on foot, and even wrote letters to help people understand how the world had changed with Jesus' death and resurrection. There were no Christian seminaries, formal teaching churches, or Bible colleges. The New Testament had not yet been compiled, much less printed in their languages!

Still, Christianity spread quickly during those days of persecution. When God's people fled for their lives, they took the good news wherever they traveled. The 12 grew to a few hundred, then to around 3,000 at Pentecost, and then to hundreds of thousands! In the A.D. fourth century, every citizen of the Roman Empire, which covered the known world, was declared a Christian.

It would probably have been unbelievable to these new Christians to hear of such growth! They were the beginners, these *slow ones* who started the movement, step by step, heart by heart, from Jerusalem to "the uttermost part of the earth" (Acts 1:8 KJV).

How did you fill in the blanks on Hebrews 5:11–12? Here are the answers. Christian describes the Hebrew Christians as slow to learn. He says, "By this time you ought to be teachers. You need someone to teach you; you need milk, not solid food." He explains: "Anyone who lives on milk, being still an infant, is not acquainted with the teaching about righteousness. But solid food is for the mature, who by constant use have trained themselves to distinguish good from evil" (Hebrews 5:13–14). For "solid food" on teaching God's Word, church culture, and life principles, read Titus 2 and *Woman to Woman: Preparing Yourself to Mentor*, pages 44–48.

My husband once said the happiest day of his life was the time our children were old enough to go somewhere at a moment's notice. He could say, "Jump in the car, kids! We're going to Grandmother's!" without packing bottles of milk and juice, a ton of diapers, jars of baby food, special blankets, a high chair, and a portable baby bed! When they could dress themselves, eat the same food we ate, and walk without our help, life with them was easier.

Babies are helpless, toothless, and speechless. Their babbling is useless, their crying senseless. They rudely burp and make other unmentionable sounds. They don't earn their keep but instead stay in bed most of the day. They take *us* for granted, thinking *they* are the center of the universe. They keep families up at night, spit up on everyone, and pitch violent tantrums. We don't tolerate this behavior in adults. Most fathers probably feel as my husband did: they can't wait for their infants to grow up! Our Father in heaven must often feel the same way about us. He longs for our maturity as children of God, knowing the difference between good and evil, teaching it, and influencing others as we grow. May we yearn not for milk but for solid food!

❧ FRIEND TO FRIEND ❧

Since Christian says your are still an infant, what does he mean? What are the characteristics of an infant?

How do these characteristics apply to you or other Christians you know?

Discuss these characteristics with your study friend.

Touch My Heart, Lord Jesus

Heavenly Father, help me not to remain a spiritual infant. I want to grow into spiritual maturity, recognizing the difference between good and evil and standing for good. Help me be a positive influence for You, to absorb Your Word and live it out daily. Forgive me when I slip back into infancy, becoming lazy in my service to You. Amen.

STUDY 13 *God's Call to Faithfulness*

HEBREWS 6:1–12

Hebrews 6

And once we've tasted heav'nly gifts,
Shared in the Holy Spirit's grace,
And tasted goodness of the Word
And powers of the coming age,

We can't go back to unsaved life;
We can't return to hardened heart;
Impossible it is, in strife
To live without our Lord, apart.

O, God, may we not ever fail
To ask forgiveness for our sin
For if we sin, oh, we disgrace
Our Lord—and crucify again!

For we are confident in You
That we can step beyond the veil,
For You have gone before, O, Christ.
We're heirs! Your hope in us instill.

—EDNA M. ELLISON, © 2002

From first through sixth grade, I attended Florida Street Elementary School in Clinton, South Carolina. Every day I walked or rode with friends across town, passing the high school, to elementary school. Near the end of the sixth grade, our family built a new home, located near Florida Street. In those days we had no middle school or junior high, so when I was 13 I attended the seventh grade at the high school, passing my old elementary school each day! On the days when we had no ride, my friends and I would complain during the entire one-mile walk. (It didn't make us feel better when our parents told us they had walked five miles to school every day in three-foot snow drifts, with wild dogs along the way!)

Leaving Elementary School

We were excited about going to high school, of course, but it made no sense for us to leave our comfort zones at the Florida Street school and walk that long trek to a new school. We had become lazy teens over the summer, and even seeing the cute boys in the eighth grade was not enough to make us happy about a brisk walk twice a day! Have you ever walked to school? Write your memories:

❧ FRIEND TO FRIEND ❧

Have you ever felt lazy and didn't exercise as you should have?

What were your concerns as you moved up to high school?

Did you have another transition in life that caused upheaval? What happened?

Share these experiences with your study friend.

As we ended Study 12, Christian, our name for the writer of Hebrews, spoke about our being baby Christians, not developing into spiritually mature adults. "By this time you ought to be teachers, [yet] you need someone to teach you the elementary truths of God's word all over again" (Hebrews 5:12). He says we should "by constant use have trained" ourselves "to distinguish good from evil" (Hebrews 5:14). In this study he gives us advice, explaining how to mature in Christ's teachings. "Therefore let us leave the elementary teachings about Christ and go on to maturity, not laying again the foundation of repentance from acts that lead to death, and of faith in God, instruction about baptisms, the laying on of hands, the resurrection of the dead, and eternal judgment. And God permitting, we will do so" (Hebrews 6:1–3).

What elementary teachings does God tell us to move past?

Why should you move past these foundational principles?

How have you grown in your understanding of God, once you understood the basics?

et FRIEND TO FRIEND et

Share your answers with your study friend.

Elementary School Items

Just as I graduated from elementary school to junior high and high school, Christians should graduate from elementary understanding and move to deeper spiritual truths. Eugene Peterson paraphrases these words from Hebrews: "So come on, let's leave the preschool fingerpainting exercises on Christ and get on with the grand work of art. Grow up in Christ. The basic foundational truths are in place: turning your back on 'salvation by self-help' and turning in trust toward God; baptismal instructions; laying on of hands; resurrection of the dead; eternal judgment. God helping us, we'll stay true to all that. But there's so much more. Let's get on with it!" (Hebrews 6:1–3 *The Message*). [Extra reading: *Baptism*: Acts 2:37–41, Acts 10:47–48, Acts 19:4–7; Romans 6:3–4; Colossians 2:11–12. *Laying on of hands*: Acts 6:6 Acts 8:17–21, Acts 19:6; 1 Timothy 4:11–14, 1 Timothy 5:22]

Then he begins the "solid food" of God's Word in the next few verses, which you may find, as I did, hard to understand at first. Consider them carefully and slowly: "It is impossible for those who have once been enlightened, who have tasted the heavenly gift, who have shared in the Holy Spirit, who have tasted the goodness of the word of God and the powers of the coming age, if they fall away, to be brought back to repentance, because to their loss they are crucifying the Son of God all over again and subjecting him to public disgrace" (Hebrews 6:4–6). Describe Christians (Hebrews 6:4–5): Those who have once been _____, who have tasted _____ who have shared _____, who have tasted the _____ of the word of _____ and the _____ of the _____ .

⊰ FRIEND TO FRIEND ⊰

Share with your study friend how you fulfill (or don't fulfill) these words.

Eugene Peterson paraphrases in *The Message*: "Once people have seen the light, gotten a taste of heaven and been part of the work of the Holy Spirit, once they've personally experienced the sheer goodness of God's Word and the powers breaking in on us—if then they turn their backs on it, washing their hands of the whole thing, well, they can't start over as if nothing happened. That's impossible. Why, they've recrucified Jesus! They've repudiated him in public!"

Christian explains two important points of *theology* (the meat, or solid food, of the gospel, understood by more mature Christians) in these verses:

1. You are saved only once. You don't need to doubt your salvation or think you constantly have to make a confession of faith to be saved from eternal damnation. If you have repented and trusted Jesus to live daily in your heart, then you will enter into heavenly rest with Him eternally. Period. You don't keep reentering that once-for-all salvation experience, except to cherish it as the most exciting thing that ever happened to you. You don't ever lose it.

2. You hurt Jesus when you doubt or backslide. Once you have been saved (recognizing your own sin and tasting the joy of being released from such slavery), if you then return to your sinful condition, it is as if you crucify Jesus again!

I believe it hurts your Lord when you disobey, lose your joy, and live as if He had not died for you. It also hurts other people around you. They notice your disobedience, lack of morals, and sadness. It subjects the name of Christ—when people have previously called you by His name, "Christian"—to public disgrace.

The Garden of God's Delight

Christian encourages us to be faithful to God's growth principles. "Land that drinks in the rain often falling on it and that produces a crop useful to those for whom it is farmed receives the blessing of God. But land that produces thorns and thistles is worthless and is in danger of being cursed. In the end it will be burned" (Hebrews 6:7–8).

Isaiah 5:1–7 compares an unfruitful vineyard that the gardener had watered, watched, and surrounded with a "hedge of protection" to a fruitful vineyard. He says "the men of Judah are the garden of his delight" (v. 7). God takes great delight in you, dear reader. You have proven—just by studying God's Word—that you do want to grow, to become ripe with God's wisdom, and to produce fruit. [Extra reading: Read Isaiah 5:11–25, selecting things you can avoid that might give God cause to be disappointed in His garden of delight.]

Christian continues with hope: "Even though we speak like this, dear friends, we are confident of better things in your case—things that accompany salvation. God is not unjust; he will not forget your work and the love you have shown him as you have helped his people and continue to help them" (Hebrews 6:9–10). What a wonderful thought: God has no memory loss (unlike me!). He will remember your work, your love for Him, and your help for other people!

❧ FRIEND TO FRIEND ❧

How does your encouraging others show your love for God?

Share ideas of things you and your study friend might do together.

Keep On Keeping On

We end this study with words of encouragement: "We want each of you to show this same diligence to the very end, in order to make your hope sure. We do not want you to become lazy, but to imitate those who through faith and patience inherit what has been promised" (Hebrews 6:11–12).

Touch My Heart, Lord Jesus

Holy Teacher, thank You for showing me that I've already made it! I don't need to keep begging for Your salvation. You have given it as a free gift. May I grow in my understanding and love for You. May I always bear the fruit of your Spirit, living in You and being diligent to the very end. Help me not to be lazy, but fruitful, growing as the garden of Your delight. All-knowing God, thank You for remembering me. Amen.

STUDY 14 *Called to God's Promise*

HEBREWS 6:13–20

AFTER A WOMEN'S RETREAT in Puerto Rico, Barbara Joiner had planned to go to the Dominican Republic to speak—and to deliver an electric mixer to missionary Sue McFadden. Although Barbara's travel agent had assured her she wouldn't need a passport, she couldn't get into the Dominican Republic without one. Her translator warned her that it would be impossible to take the gifts, which would be mistaken for black-market items.

Finding she needed an attorney, Barbara called a local seminary and asked if they knew one. They didn't, but someone was walking down a nearby hallway, and when they checked, it was a Baptist attorney! He soon called Barbara (speaking only Spanish!), and they agreed to meet at a certain street corner, where he gave her an impressive document.

At the ticket counter the next day, an agent accepted her document in lieu of a passport, clicked his heels, and saluted. Then he carried her luggage, escorting her on the plane. Barbara says, "I sensed for the first time how Abraham must have felt going out he knew not where." Later she deplaned—with 12 soldiers snapping to attention and the pilot carrying her luggage to the terminal! Giving a queenly wave, she was escorted to a reception room, where she met the missionaries. Her giant document, signed by "El Presidente," was a royal voucher that granted her unlimited access!

God's promise today will also be honored. As sovereign ruler, He has the authority to grant any promise because He is Creator, owner of everything! Jesus says, "I tell you the truth, my Father will give you whatever you ask in my name. Until now you have not asked for anything in my name. Ask and you will receive, and your joy will be complete. . . . Take heart! I have overcome the world" (John 16:23–24, 33). In today's study we will explore an incredible promise from Almighty God!

Do you believe God will give you whatever you ask in Jesus' name?

Have you asked in His name?

After you asked and received, was your joy complete—or has it faded?

What does Jesus mean: "I have overcome the world"?

❧ FRIEND TO FRIEND ❧

Share answers to these questions with your study friend.

First, Christian, our name for the Hebrews writer, reminds us of the Old Testament promise God gave to Abraham: "When God made his promise to Abraham, since there was no one greater for him to swear by, he swore by himself, saying, 'I will surely bless you and give you many descendants.' And so after waiting patiently, Abraham received what was promised" (Hebrews 6:13–15).

It's Bigger than All of Us

Saying Abraham waited patiently is a grand understatement! God told him to move to an unknown land. God said, " 'Leave your country, your people and your father's household and go to the land I will show you. I will make you into a great nation and I will bless you; I will make your name great, and you will be a blessing. I will bless those who bless you, and whoever curses you I will curse; and all peoples on earth will be blessed through you.' So Abram left, as the Lord had told him" (Genesis 12:1–4).

You remember the story: Abram and Sarai had no children. Over the course of their journey, God changed their names to Abraham and Sarah, making them father of nations and mother of nations. At age 90 Sarah conceived, and Isaac was born. What a remarkable miracle! This story demonstrates the promises of a loving God—blessings, no matter what.

Then a strange episode happened. God did the unthinkable: He told Abraham to sacrifice Isaac. In the deserted place where Abraham prepared to sacrifice Isaac, destroying his only hope for legitimate heirs, God stopped him, providing a stray ram for the sacrifice. Abraham had been tested, and God then renewed His vows. Christian quotes from the end of this scene recorded in Genesis: "'I swear by myself, declares the Lord, that because you have done this and have not withheld your son, your only son, I will surely bless you and make your descendants as numerous as the stars in the sky and as the sand on the seashore. . . . Through your offspring all nations on earth will be blessed, because you have obeyed me'" (Genesis 22:16–18).

As he recalls the Old Testament story, Christian says: "Men swear by someone greater than themselves, and the oath confirms what is said and puts an end to all argument. Because God wanted to make the unchanging nature of his purpose very clear to the heirs of what was promised, he confirmed it with an oath" (Hebrews 6:16–17).

According to Hebrews 6, why do men swear?

By what/ whom do they swear?

Why did God confirm his promise to Abraham with an oath?

✥ FRIEND TO FRIEND ✥

Share your feelings about swearing with your study friend.

A young woman from Korea amazed me with her knowledge of America. She said, "As a little girl, I learned a lot about your country from the GIs who fought in my country. I soon learned they were godly men." I sat smugly thinking of how righteous our nation was, until she said, "*God* was an everyday word they used all the time! After I moved here to worship, I learned those men where cussing. You say, 'calling God's name in vain,' don't you?" What she took as worshipful behavior was cursing behavior! It broke my heart to know that our nation sends out representatives to share curses with the rest of the world.

In a recent popular movie the main character is magically translated from the mid-twentieth century to the present time. His newfound friends take him to a movie to show him current culture. When he hears profanity, he screams and runs out of the theater. How about you? Are you offended when you hear misguided oaths, or have you become so accustomed to them that you ignore them?

Have you become immune to bad language you hear on television or other entertainment sources?

List a few things you can do to move closer to purity.

✥ FRIEND TO FRIEND ✥

Is profanity a problem with you or your family?

How should God's name be used?

How can you be sure you please Him in the way you use His name?

Share your ideas with your study friend.

When God used an oath, He used it properly: "God did this [swore an oath] so that, by two unchangeable things in which it is impossible for God to lie, we who have fled to take hold of the hope offered to us may be greatly encouraged. We have this hope as an anchor for the soul, firm and secure" (Hebrews 6:18–19).

Think through this passage. God's word is true. He cannot lie. However, in case someone may doubt His word is truth, He confirms His promise—backs it up—with an oath. This oath is also guaranteed truth. You now have two unchangeable truths. You have fled [rushed] to take hold of the hope of God's truth. God encourages you through this great hope! Hope is a firm, secure anchor for your soul!

Eugene Peterson paraphrases, "When God made his promise to Abraham, he backed it to the hilt, putting his own reputation on the line." As Christian says, we can rush to take hold of the hope God offers us, greatly encouraged, anchored securely in life, because God Himself has given us His promise!

Access Behind the Veil

Christian explains further: "It [our hope] enters the inner sanctuary behind the curtain, where Jesus, who went before us, has entered on our behalf. He has become a high priest forever, in the order of Melchizedek" (Hebrews 6:19–20). In these verses, Christian refers to the embroidered curtain, or veil, which divided the tabernacle's Holy Place, where the priests entered, from the Most Holy Place, where only the high priest could enter (and then only at special times). The veil is described in Exodus 26:31–33:

> "Make a curtain of blue, purple and scarlet yarn and finely twist-ed linen, with cherubim worked into it by a skilled craftsman. Hang it with gold hooks on four posts of acacia wood overlaid with gold and standing on four silver bases. Hang the curtain from the clasps and place the ark of the Testimony behind the curtain. The curtain will separate the Holy Place from the Most Holy Place."

We'll learn more about these two areas of the tabernacle in later studies.

A Better Promise

Look back at Hebrews 6:20. God's promise is culminated in the resurrection of Jesus Christ. Just as the high priest entered the tabernacle's Most Holy Place, where the ark symbolizing the presence of God rested, Jesus entered into the presence of God when He was raised from the dead and then ascended into heaven, where He waits for us. At His death, the veil was ripped open: "And when Jesus had cried out again in a loud voice, he gave up his spirit. At that moment the curtain of the temple was torn in two from top to bottom" (Matthew 27:50–51). Through Jesus, we have access through the veil to the actual presence of God! His presence today can rest not in an ark, but within us!

Have you ever experienced direct promises from God? What happened?

Have you ever doubted His goodness, but were surprised by His faithfulness?

What does the ripping of the veil mean to you personally?

❧ FRIEND TO FRIEND ❧

Share your hope with your study friend.

Fulfilling the Better Promise

When Jesus entered heaven on our behalf, Christian says, He became a high priest forever—not a physical high priest whose body goes into the place of God's presence, but a spiritual high priest whose Spirit leads us into His presence. In Study 15, we'll learn more about the "forever priest," Melchizedek, and learn how Jesus fulfills the better promise!

Touch My Heart, Lord Jesus

Almighty God, I praise Your powerful name. Your words of truth give me an anchor for my soul. I feel safe and secure because of the hope I have in You. Thank You for blessings and for answered prayer. Thank You for providing Your Son, Jesus, as my entry into heaven. May I respect Your holy name and rejoice a I hope in Your promises. Amen.

STUDY 15 *The One Who Calls Me*
HEBREWS 7:1–22

Hebrews 7
The Bible says in Abram's day
This timely message was foretold:
The Savior would soon lead the way—
God gave a promise of pure gold.

From Judah, Ruth, and David came
Our great High Priest forever more!
His sacrifice was once, the same
For all eternity: the Door!

No other sacrifice, no law,
No heritage nor lineage pure
Was needed; only Jesus, called,
Obeyed, and suffering, endured.
We have the promise by God's oath
Who did appoint the Son, I AM;
And now forever better, both
The Father and the perfect Lamb.

—EDNA M. ELLISON, © 2002

We left Study 14 with Christian, our name for the author of Hebrews, repeating the name Melchizedek from Genesis 14:17–20 and Psalm 110:4. In Hebrews 7:1–2, he gives a brief overview of the man he first mentioned in Hebrews 5 (Study 11): "This Melchizedek was king of Salem and priest of God Most High. He met Abraham returning from the defeat of the kings and blessed him, and Abraham gave him a tenth of everything."

Kingly High Priest
Read carefully Christian's identification of Melchizedek: "First, his name means 'king of righteousness'; then also, 'king of Salem' means 'king of peace.' Without father or mother, without genealogy, without beginning of days or end of life, like the Son of God he remains a priest forever. Just think how great he was: Even the patriarch Abraham gave him a tenth of the plunder! Now the law requires the descendants of Levi who become priests to collect a tenth from the people—that is, their brothers—even though their brothers are descended from Abraham" (Hebrews 7:2–5).

Read Hebrews 7: 2–4 and identify Melchizedek by filling in the following blanks:

His name means "king of _____."

"King of Salem" means "king of _____."

Without father or _____.

Without _____.

Without beginning of days or _____.

Like the Son of God, he is a priest _____.

Think how _____ He was!

Christian identifies Melchizedek as "king of righteousness," and "king of peace," two descriptions we use for Jesus. He also indicated Melchizedek had no known earthly family: "without father or mother, without genealogy." He seemed immortal, "without beginning of days or end of life." Christian says, "like the Son of God, he is a priest forever," a definite reference to Jesus.

After this description, Christian draws an interesting parallel: Melchizedek received ten percent (a tithe) of the plunder (gold, jewelry, other items gathered in a holy war) from the patriarch Abraham. In Moses' day, God appointed the Levites (descendants of Levi, Abraham's great-grandson) as a priestly family. They received no property in the promised land, Canaan, after their exodus out of Egypt, but instead received ten percent of the income of all the other Israelites (silver, gold, livestock, fruit, or other things), who willingly gave their possessions to take care of their priests—their worship leaders. It was unusual for Abraham to give Melchizedek the tithe, because their encounter happened years before the Levites were even born—before the tithe was set!

Christian explains: "This man, however, did not trace his descent from Levi, yet he collected a tenth from Abraham and blessed him who had the promises. And without doubt the lesser person is blessed by the greater" (Hebrews 7:6–7). Common sense tells us that a lesser person is blessed by a greater one. Abraham, the richer one, the receiver of God's promises, the patriarch of a great nation to come, a courageous adventurer and warrior, was—in short—a great man. In this case, who was it, Abraham or Melchizedek, who got the blessing? It was Abraham. Then logic follows that Melchizedek must have been the greater of the two. Here was a priest forever, a man greater than the famous patriarch Abraham!

A New High Priest

Next, Christian contrasts the Old Testament law about Levite priests (and Abraham) to the New Testament living law about Jesus, our High Priest (and Melchizedek): "In the one case, the tenth is collected by men who die; but in the other case, by him who is declared to be living. One might even say that Levi, who collects the tenth, paid the tenth through Abraham, because when Melchizedek met Abraham, Levi was still in the body of his ancestor" (Hebrews 7:8–10).

Since Levi was not born until after Abraham's life, you can stretch a point and say that Levi, Abraham's great-grandson, paid the tenth to Melchizedek, since his DN A came from Abraham, who did pay the tenth. Can you stretch your imagination even further and say that the New Testament Levites (those living as priests in Christian's day) who collected tithes (notice present tense: "collects" v. 9) from the people, were less than the New Testament Melchizedek, Jesus (since Melchizedek was a foreshadowing of Jesus; a prototype like the suffering servant, the good shepherd, the prince of peace, the sacrificial lamb, and other symbolic figures who pointed people to Jesus)?

Authority	Life	Pattern	Reality	Sacrifice	Power
Old Testament (Physical Law)	Soon Dead	Abraham	Levite priests	Lambs	Lesser
New Testament (Spiritual Law)	Ever-living	Melchizedek	Jesus, High Priest	His Body	Greater

Why do you think Christian, who lived in the first century, says Levi collects (present tense) the tithe, when Levi lived centuries before Christian?

Why do you think he says Levi paid the tenth to Melchizedek, in the days of Abraham, who lived many years before Levi?

Does this seem "too far out" to believe?

God's goodness transcends time. Spiritual truth goes beyond physical explanations. Melchizedek lived even before the priestly rituals began. For centuries the Jewish people had pointed to Melchizedek as an example of an exception to the rule, an outstanding "great one" who gave a spiritual blessing. Abraham had respected his spiritual greatness and paid tribute to him. Christian saw, as Abraham saw in faith, that priestly rituals do not save us, but Jesus, far greater than even the greatest earthly priest, does.

✥ FRIEND TO FRIEND ✥

Share with your study friend your ideas on God transcending earthly time.

A Perfect Priest

"If perfection could have been attained through the Levitical priesthood (for on the basis of it the law was given to the people), why was there still need for another priest to come—one in the order of Melchizedek, not in the order of Aaron? For when there is a change of the priesthood, there must also be a change of the law" (Hebrews 7:11–12).

To understand these verses, it's helpful to know that Aaron (along with Moses, his brother), was a Levite (Exodus 6:16–20). Christian poses a pivotal question: if perfection could have been accomplished through the mediation of priests, why did Jesus need to come?

Write in your own words why it was necessary for Jesus to come to earth and become your high priest:

As your high priest, what does He provide?

As a Christian, how have you experienced His changing your life?

Share your answers to these questions with your study friend.

There's no doubt about it; Christian believed that the Levitical priesthood did *not* attain perfection; in other words, Levites were just humans who offered sacrifices and gave earthly blessings upon other humans. In fact, Hebrews 5:3 reminds us they had to offer sacrifices for their own sins also. There was a need, he said, for a high priest in the order of Melchizedek, not in the order of Aaron (or the Levites). Jesus, like Melchizedek, was an exception to the rule: He would bring everlasting, not temporary, salvation. If this "better priest" was an exception to the rule, then maybe the rule needed changing.

Look back at verse 12: A change of priesthood required a change of law. The time had come for the Old Testament law to be renewed in a new covenant, or New Testament. Christian says, "He of whom these things are said belonged to a different tribe, and no one from that tribe has ever served at the altar" (Hebrews 7:13). Jesus was not a descendent of Levi. His mother, Mary (and his stepfather, Joseph), descended from Judah, not from Levi. [Extra reading—genealogies: Matthew 1:2–17; Luke 3:23–38; 1 Chronicles 3:1–24; Isaiah 11:1–2, 10]

Christian says, "For it is clear that our Lord descended from Judah, and in regard to that tribe Moses said nothing about priests. And what we have said is even more clear if another priest like Melchizedek appears, one who has become a priest not on the basis of a regulation as to his ancestry but on the basis of the power of an indestructible life" (Hebrews 7:14–16).

High Priest Forever

In verse 17 Christian quotes Psalm 110:4, "For it is declared: 'You are a priest forever, in the order of Melchizedek.' The former regulation is set aside because it was weak and useless (for the law made nothing perfect)" (Hebrews 7:17–19).

The better hope offers a better covenant: "And a better hope is introduced, by which we draw near to God. And it was not without an oath! Others became priests without any oath, but he became a priest with an oath when God said to him: 'The Lord has sworn and will not change his mind: "You are a priest forever." ' Because of this oath, Jesus has become the guarantee of a better covenant" (Hebrews 7:19–22). Jesus says, "Do not think that I have come to abolish the Law or the Prophets; I have not come to abolish them but to fulfill them" (Matthew 5:17). What a Savior! Jesus calls you with His promise into the presence of the Living God, and forever holds open the door to the throne of grace.

Touch My Heart, Lord Jesus

O High Priest forever, thank You for calling me, one of the lesser ones, to follow You through the veil, into the presence of the Living God. Help me realize that my salvation and happiness do not depend on earthly things, but on heavenly blessings. Lord, You are my everlasting Savior, one with sure promises and a better covenant. Amen.

UNIT 4 *A New Covenant*

GODLY WOMAN, garden of His delight, prepare your heart for this unit filled with deep truth. He loves you and wants you to understand remarkable things you do not yet know. God revealed to His people—His delight—something new! Don't you feel a tingle of excitement when you know a new thing or new event is coming? The following pages will lead you through the door to truth as you learn about getting a home permanent, making copies from the Original Master, and mediating a win-win situation. You'll also find out where "Jesus Saves" comes from (not from a barn roof!) and how to inherit a new heart. As a Christian woman, I know you'll want to learn more about the interior decorating in the Holy of Holies!

Sound like fun? I hope it is. But more than that, I hope you'll discover a new relationship with Jesus, a new covenant that changes your life. Ready? Let's begin!

STUDY 16 *The Power of a Permanent Priesthood*
HEBREWS 7:23–28

WHEN MY DAUGHTER, Patsy, was born, she was bald. I had hoped for a few curls, but would have been pleased with just a few stray hairs! We have pictures of her first Christmas celebration with a small bow taped to her head—not a pretty sight! By age five, she had grown a few strands of hair, but they were limp and sparse. Our doctor said nothing was wrong with her health, but I was concerned. It didn't help that all her friends showed up at church on Sunday mornings with their thick curls bouncing, and she wished her hair would bounce! Before the days of hot curling irons and hair spray, we began a ritual of Saturday hair care. I washed her hair carefully and rolled it in curlers. We let it dry all day, and late Saturday I'd unroll it, and it went straight immediately. I bought a set of sponge curlers, and she wore them all day Saturday and went to bed with them that night. On Sunday mornings, those curls bounced, but by the time we arrived at church all curls were gone. Poof! Cinderella had changed from the princess into the stepsister in the ashes.

One day at a local department store, Patsy saw a home permanent. "Mommy, Betsy got one of those to give her some curls!"

"She did?" I fingered the box. Hmmm. Simple instructions. Easy to do in one afternoon. Guaranteed to give a permanent curl. Sounds great! We planned a home beauty shop experience the next day. As Patsy sat under the smelly liquid I had poured over her hair, neither of us could wait to see the finished product. Finally, the time was up, and I began to unroll her hair.

Nothing.

The hair looked exactly as it had before we started: limp, thin, and hanging like the wispy threads of a spider web! I was so disappointed I cried, but I didn't let Patsy see me. That night my husband, listening to me complain, said, "Just be patient. Remember, some things marked 'permanent' are not really permanent." He had just spent a fortune on "permanent" windshield wipers for the car that had fallen apart in a hard rain.

Gradually Patsy's hair became longer and thicker, and today she has beautiful hair, but we still drag out the old family photos from time to time and remember the permanent that was not permanent.

Have you ever had a bad hair day that ruined your attitude?

Have you ever had a permanent?

Have you ever had a home permanent?

Have you ever wished life were more permanent (that made-up beds stayed neat, that dusted tables remained dust-free, that your relationships with loved ones were permanent, etc.)? Explain.

How is Jesus' permanence a solid hope for you?

⮞❦ FRIEND TO FRIEND ❦⮜

Share you answers to these questions with your study friend.

Perfect Lord

One of the characteristics of Melchizedek that Christian, our name for the Hebrews author, admired was his unchanging timelessness. He was permanent. Compared to the Levitical priests, who died, he calls Melchizedek a priest forever. He ascribes that same characteristic to Jesus: "Now there have been many of those priests, since death prevented them from continuing in office; but because Jesus lives forever, he has a permanent priesthood" (Hebrews 7:23–24). Few things in life are permanent, but Jesus is definitely permanent. He defeated death on the Cross and rose for eternity.

This permanence qualifies Jesus to save you: "Therefore he is able to save completely those who come to God through him, because he always lives to intercede for them. Such a high priest meets our need—one who is holy, blameless, pure, set apart from sinners, exalted about the heavens" (Hebrews 7:25–26).

Read the following words about Jesus and tell how Christian describes each. Here's the first answer:
1. Perfectly permanent (v. 24): *lives forever*
2. Perfect power (v. 25):
3. Perfect salvation:
4. Perfect opportunity (for all):
5. Perfectly everlasting:
6. Perfect intercessor:
7. Perfect provider (v. 26):
8. Perfect righteousness:
9. Perfect innocence:
10. Perfect purity:
11. Perfect uniqueness:
12. Perfect position:

Have you ever read *Jesus Saves* on a barn or a bumper sticker? This saying came from Hebrews 7:25. Sometimes people say these two words are just "churchy talk" that average folks don't understand; but however you say it, the gospel is contained in these two words. *Jesus Saves* is true—it's the heart of the gospel, the good news. These short verses (7:24–26) explain how perfect the good news is! It centers on Jesus, who has these characteristics:

Perfectly permanent (v. 24):	*lives forever*
Perfect power (v. 25):	*able*
Perfect salvation:	*to save completely*
Perfect opportunity (for all):	*those who come*
Perfectly everlasting:	*always lives*

Perfect intercessor:	*to intercede for them*
Perfect provider (v. 26):	*meets our need*
Perfect righteousness:	*holy*
Perfect innocence:	*blameless*
Perfect purity:	*pure*
Perfect uniqueness:	*set apart from sinners*
Perfect position:	*exalted above the heavens*

✣ FRIEND TO FRIEND ✣

Have you ever seen "Jesus Saves" on the side of a barn or on a bumper sticker? How do you honestly feel when you see these words?

Do such words cheapen the gospel or validate it for those who may never read God's Word or go to a church?

Look up *finite* and *infinite* in a dictionary. How do you qualify as finite? How does Jesus qualify as infinite?

Isn't it amazing that your Lord, who lives forever, is *able* (a powerful word to consider) to save completely those who come (you and me—and even the worst murderer in the world, if he comes to Jesus)? "Always lives to intercede for them" indicates the complete unselfishness of your Lord, who wants to be your advocate, your public relations representative, your mediator, who puts you in right relationship with God. He provides for your needs—whatever they are. He *can* because He has perfect character as a resource: He's holy, blameless, and pure!

Set apart from the rest of the sinners you know (and even you and me, who are sinners), He is now exalted above the heavens! This infinite passage contains more than my finite brain can comprehend! Pause for a moment now and praise God for the infinite Jesus!

Lord of Perfect Sacrifice

After the magnificent passage above, Christian begins to contrast two things. On one side stand the priests; on the other stands the infinite, perfect Jesus, our high priest: "Unlike the other high priests, he does not need to offer sacrifices day after day, first for his own sins, and then for the sins of the people. He sacrificed for their sins once for all when he offered himself. For the law appoints as high priests men who are weak; but the oath, which came after the law, appointed the Son, who has been made perfect forever" (Hebrews 7:27–28).

He contrasts:

the Hebrew high priests	with	Jesus, the high priest
daily animal sacrifices	with	no animal sacrifice needed today
priests' own sins	with	Jesus: no sin
people's sins	with	a once-for-all sacrifice—Jesus
law	with	oath of God (law fulfilled)
weak	with	strong
sinful	with	perfect
daily	with	forever

What a momentous shift in history. The world moved from B.C. to A.D.; the law melted away as spiritual law was written on our hearts! No animal sacrifices are ever needed again. As we have studied Hebrews verse by verse, we see the theme of "better" coming to the surface. Our Lord *is* better; He's *superior* to the priests! If you skimmed over the poem at the beginning of Study 15, reflect once more:

> No smelly sacrifice, no law,
> No heritage nor lineage pure
> Was needed; only Jesus, called,
> Obeyed, and suffering, endured.
>
> We have the promise by God's oath
> Who did appoint the Son, I AM;
> And now forever better, both
> The Father and the perfect Lamb.

Jesus is forever better, that is, better than anything we could ever wish for. And His superiority lasts forever! If you know it, sing the hymn that says, "I'd rather have Jesus than silver or gold." Would you rather have Jesus than any wealth or satisfaction? What would you rather have, once and for all? In Study 19, you'll find more about Jesus' once-for-all sacrifice.

Touch My Heart, Lord Jesus

O God, whose oath, my personal promise from You, gives me hope of eternity, thank You for the perfect high priest, the infinite Jesus, who is a permanent security in my life. His love and sacrifice for me is more than I can comprehend! Help me to understand how Jesus saves and to share that truth with others around me. Amen.

STUDY 17 *Lord, Please Sit at the Mediation Table*

HEBREWS 8:1–7

Hebrews 8
The point of all His Word is this:
The Lamb sits high on heaven's throne,
New tabernacle, not amiss,
In all true power: Him alone!

And our high priests, or pastors, true
Serve as a sanctuary sure,
But only copy, shadow, too,
Of what in heaven does endure.

God writes His laws upon your heart;
And He will be your God, and we
Will be His people! Now we start!
Our Lord says now, "They'll *all* know me."

"For I'll recall their sin no more,
And I'll forgive them, one by one."
Old covenants by Jesus tore . . .
Alive! New Cov'nant has begun!

—EDNA M. ELLISON, © 2002

I travel often on airplanes, sitting next to strangers, with whom I talk as if I'd known them all my life. It's amazing what strangers share when they think they'll never see you again! I like to call it "midair therapy"! Sometimes they're on their way to a funeral, a job interview, a divorce hearing, or some other thing that opens them to a Christian witness.

A year ago I rode next to a man who said he was a negotiator, or mediator. He said he found out what each of the two parties really wanted and then met their needs around the mediation table in a win-win situation. Usually each party offered something the other wanted, and they eventually signed a contract with their solemn promises.

Lord, Please Sit at the Mediation Table

The role of an Old Testament high priest was also that of mediator. He was the go-between, mediating between a just God and a sinful person. Christian explains how Jesus fulfills that role: "The point of what we are saying is this: We do have such a high priest, who sat down at the right hand of the throne of the Majesty in heaven, and who serves in the sanctuary, the true tabernacle set up by the Lord, not by man. Every high priest is appointed to offer both gifts and sacrifices, and so it was necessary for this one also to have something to offer" (Hebrews 8:1–3). Jesus is not just *a* mediator; He is *the only* mediator between you and God (1 Timothy 2:5)—and He has much to offer!

As Christian says, today Jesus sits at the right hand of the Majesty's (God's) throne in heaven. This is a strategic position, a preferred seat at the mediation table. In Bible times, the right hand was the righteous hand, and the left hand the less-than-perfect one. Today in Korea, the left hand is the "bathroom hand," and is not shown at the dinner table, much less used!

Once the disciples understood the reality of Jesus sitting with God in heaven, James and John asked, "Let one of us sit at your right and the other at your left in your glory" (Mark 10:37). Jesus made it clear that whoever wants to be great would be a servant, not a ruler: "Whoever wants to be first must be slave of all. For even the Son of Man did not come to be served, but to serve, and to give his life as a ransom for many" (Mark 10:44–45).

❧ FRIEND TO FRIEND ❧

According to Hebrews 8:1, who is your high priest?

Exactly where is He sitting?

Where does He serve?

What does He offer?

Christian also makes it clear that Jesus is serving in heaven. Look back at Hebrews 8:1–3. He "serves in the sanctuary, the true tabernacle set up by the Lord, not by man" (8:2). The tabernacle set up by Moses to hold the ark of the covenant was a flimsy cloth tent hanging on poles, moved around the dessert as the Israelites moved. In contrast, "the true tabernacle set up by the Lord" is in heaven, the perfect place of worship. Like Jesus (see Study 16), it is permanent!

God's Word describes the ark as a chest of acacia wood, two and a half cubits long, a cubit and a half wide, and a cubit and a half high. It was overlaid with pure gold, inside and out, with gold molding (Exodus 25:10–11). John says in the Book of Revelation: "Then I saw a new heaven. . . . The city was laid out like a square, as long as it was wide. . . . 12,000 stadia in length [about 1,400 miles], and as wide and high as it is long. . . . The wall was made of jasper, and the city of pure gold" (Revelation 21:1, 16, 18). We can see these as two gold rectangles or cubes, both fitting places for the presence of God. The ark was wood covered in gold, but heaven is pure gold; it is the better thing, the perfect cube! A priest served at the ark, but Jesus serves in heaven; the better high priest in the better sanctuary—the better place of worship for all of us!

In Hebrews 8:3, Christian compares the two negotiators at the mediation table: "Every high priest is appointed to offer both gifts and sacrifices, and so it was necessary for this one also to have something to offer." Does Jesus have anything to offer you?

Jesus has given me so many gifts I can't count them all! How about you? He gives me peace, the dignity of the Spirit, a sense of belonging, intimacy with my Savior, and most of all, hope for eternal life. When I die I won't just rot in a grave. I believe my soul will go to heaven; I'll have life after death because Jesus promised! At the mediation table He promised you that, too. He also sacrificed three times: First, He sacrificed His position in heaven to come to earth, with sin and trouble. Second, He gave His time on earth to heal the sick, raise the dead, and forgive the wicked. Third, and most important, He sacrificed His own life—suffering blood, sweat, and tears—to die for your sins and mine.

❧ FRIEND TO FRIEND ❧

What does Jesus have to offer?

Gifts:

Sacrifices:

Share your answers with your study friend.

The Original, Not a Copy

Jesus is the original, like the "master" document is to an overhead transparency. "If he were on earth, he would not be a priest, for there are already men who offer the gifts prescribed by the law. They serve at a sanctuary that is a copy and shadow of what is in heaven. This is why Moses was warned when he was about to build the tabernacle: 'See to it that you make everything according to the pattern shown you on the mountain' " (Hebrews 8:4–5). On Mount Sinai, God gave Moses a glimpse of heaven when He gave him the tabernacle plans (Exodus 25:8–9, 40)—with the ark of the covenant in the Most Holy Place included—so much like the image of heaven given to John in Revelation.

Christian says an earthly priest serves at a sanctuary that is (1) a copy, (2) a shadow, and (3) a pattern of heaven. As heaven is superior to churches (or tabernacles), so Jesus is superior to our earthly clergy. Furthermore, Jesus' ministry is founded on superior promises: "But the ministry Jesus has received is as superior to theirs as the covenant of which he is mediator is superior to the old one, and it is founded on better promises" (Hebrews 8:6).

Here's the first hint of something wrong in chapter 8: Christian says, "For if there had been nothing wrong with that first covenant, no place would have been sought for another" (Hebrews 8:7). Think deeply about this verse: Was God wrong to give this first covenant? If the law was God's pattern, if Moses truly had been given God's plan for redemption, then how could it be wrong? Could it be that the law, the old covenant, was not perfect?

God wasn't the author of sin, yet He knew Satan, a fallen angel, had brought sin, rebellion against God, into the world. God understood our sinful nature. When He gave the Ten Commandments and the Levitical law, it was perfect, for everything He does is perfect.

However, *the way people followed the law* was not perfect. We are wrong:

we misuse laws God gives us. God knew all along it was impossible for us to keep every rule in that pattern set for us. He knows *your* frailties. And here's the best part: He loves you anyway.

We'll study more about the reasons for God's law in Study 18.

Paul says in Ephesians 1:3–4a, "Praise be to the God and Father of our Lord Jesus Christ, who has blessed us in the heavenly realms with every spiritual blessing in Christ. For he chose us in him before the creation of the world to be holy and blameless in his sight." Good news! Jesus provides the way into the heavenly realms!

The greatest blessing is that your presence in heaven has nothing to do with your behavior. Your salvation doesn't depend on it. Jesus broke the pattern. He mediated for you a win-win situation. He chose you; and He's the only entrance into heaven.

✣ FRIEND TO FRIEND ✣

Can God be wrong? Is it His nature to make mistakes or lie?

Why do you think God gave the Ten Commandments and the old covenant rules if he knew men and women would break those laws?

Share with your study friend.

Touch My Heart, Lord Jesus
Mediator of the new covenant, thank You for Your promises. Thank You for access to God as my original high priest, not a copy. Bless me with the blessings of heaven, Lord, and help me understand that I don't have to be good or work my way to heaven. All I need is getting my spirit right with Yours as we each sign the covenant together. Amen.

STUDY 18 *I've Inherited a New Heart*

HEBREWS 8:8–13

HANGING OVER MY MOTHER'S BED for years was a picture of footprints in the sand. The words below the picture told of a man complaining because he had to walk alone during a tough period of his life. When he got to heaven, fearing God had abandoned him to walk alone, he asked God why the double footprints became single footprints during the hard times. God replied that during the troubled period the prints were His own. The man was unable to walk, and God had carried him through the sand. Without your knowing it, God has probably carried you through many tough times. (Yes, even through those in which you cried and complained that God didn't care!) God always cares for us, and He carries us on eagles' wings.

We left Hebrews in Study 17 with Christian, our name for the Hebrews writer, declaring the old covenant an imperfect law. Today's study will explore new exciting ways in which God touches our hearts!

"But God found fault with the people and said: 'The time is coming, declares the Lord, when I will make a new covenant with the house of Israel and with the house of Judah. It will not be like the covenant I made with their forefathers when I took them by the hand to lead them out of Egypt, because they did not remain faithful to my covenant, and I turned away from them, declares the Lord'" (Hebrews 8:8–9).

God had been patient with the Israelites. What an opportunity He had offered them!

> "Then Moses went up to God, and the Lord called to him from the mountain and said, 'This is what you are to . . . tell the people of Israel: "You yourselves have seen what I did to Egypt, and how I carried you on eagles' wings and brought you to myself. Now if you obey me fully and keep my covenant, then out of all nations you will be my treasured possession. Although the whole earth is mine, you will be for me a kingdom of priests and a holy nation"'"
>
> (Exodus 19:3–6).

If God gave us an opportunity to be a holy nation today, could we, would we, do it?

The most loving words in this passage are that God carried them and brought them to Himself. As a loving Father, He answered their need for deliverance from slavery in Egypt and then carried them in His arms to safety. In return, He asked two things: obey and keep My covenant. He also promised to make them His treasured possession, a kingdom of priests, a holy nation.

❧ FRIEND TO FRIEND ❧

What two commands did God give the Israelites?

What did He promise in return?

Share with your study friend.

Internal Heart, Not External Regulations

The Israelites promised, "We will do everything the Lord has said" (Exodus 19:8), but their promise was not as good as their word. On the contrary, God's promise was as good as His word—perfect and permanent: " 'This is the covenant I will make with the house of Israel after that time, declares the Lord. I will put my laws in their minds and write them on their hearts. I will be their God, and they will be my people' " (Hebrews 8:10). This is a wonderful comparison of God's laws: the old external, written in stone, and the new internal, written in their hearts. Just as the Levites, Abraham's descendants, inherited the old covenant, you personally have inherited the exciting new covenant: read Hebrews 8:10 again and hear His tender words as He gives you four promises: (1) to put His laws in *your* mind, (2) to write them on *your* heart, (3) to be *your* God, and (4) to claim *you* as one of His people! Celebrate your personal covenant with Him now, in a moment of praise.

Not a Secondhand Lord

In Study 17 we explored the question "Why did God give the Ten Commandments and the old covenant rules if He knew we'd break them?" Galatians 3:19, 23–24 sheds light on that question: "What, then, was the purpose of the law? It was added because of transgressions until the Seed [Jesus] to whom the promise referred had come. . . . we were held prisoners by the law, locked up until faith should be revealed. So the law was put in charge to lead us to Christ, that we might be justified [made right with God] by faith." The Book of Hebrews adds these words from God: "'No longer will a man teach his neighbor, or a man his brother, saying, "Know the Lord," because they will all know me, from the least of them to the greatest'" (Hebrews 8:11). Aren't you glad you don't need someone to tell you everything God says? You can read His Word and hear Him teach you Himself. Aren't you glad you don't need some human to judge you and condemn you? You don't need a secondhand Lord! From the least to the greatest, we can treasure God's spiritual laws in our own hearts because we know Him.

Then God gives you the words that should make your pulse race: "'For I will forgive their wickedness and will remember their sins no more'" (Hebrews 8:12).

Hallelujah! When I think of all the mean, wicked—just plain ornery—things I've done, I can hardly believe that God has forgiven me and forgotten my sins! He has (1) forgiven—like applying correction fluid to an original master—wiping my heart clean. Then (2) He forgot what was under the correction fluid! These two promises added to the first four (in v. 10) make a Sacred Six I can depend on.

❧ FRIEND TO FRIEND ❧

According to Hebrews 8:10–12, what are God's six promises?

1.

2.

3.

4.

5.

6.

Sacred Six Replace the Old Ten

Christian says, "By calling this covenant 'new,' he has made the first one obsolete; and what is obsolete and aging will soon disappear" (Hebrews 8:13). What a change! The law on stone faded away, allowing Jesus' new spiritual law to be written on your heart. It supersedes the Levitical law. You are no longer a slave. You are free! No more guilt or blood or sacrifice or sin. Only love and absolution and forgiveness and a promise you'll never forget!

Touch My Heart, Lord Jesus

O caring and carrying God, take me by the hand the way You did the Israelites. Thank You for carrying me during the tough times of life, Lord. Forgive me for not seeing Your care every step of the way. Thank You for giving me an inheritance: personal promises to hold in my heart. May I be faithful to treasure Your forgiveness and Your Holy Spirit daily. Amen.

STUDY 19 *I've Gone from Death to Life*
HEBREWS 9:1–10

Hebrews 8
The Old, with regulations hard;
The New, His voice in tender part;
Indwelling is the Holy Bard
Who writes His poetry in your heart!

To cleanse our consciences and then
To show us all the upward way;
To give us hope—women and men,
To serve the Living God always.

Consider this: when someone dies,
We prove that death has taken place.
Heirs find the will that certifies
Their loved one left them gifts of grace.

And so is certified our Lord.
Until He comes, with diadem,
(Once and for all He died for us).
Remembering, we wait for Him.

—EDNA M. ELLISON, © 2002

When I was a little girl, I learned how intelligent my father was. He always used logic to prove his points, and he was masterful at it. With his brilliance, he could have been a court lawyer! Daddy always used logic, going point by point until he wore us all down. Mother never stood a chance to win an argument—and neither did my siblings, nor I! Daddy was always right. As I grew older, I learned to appreciate a good man's logic. My childhood training in how to think helped me do well on tests and solve problems logically. It helped me understand the logical plan of salvation that's so disarming in its simplicity that people skip right over the basic truth: We can go from death to life because of God's love.

✣ FRIEND TO FRIEND ✣

Have you ever admired someone's ability at logic? What happened?

How could you use your logic to support the claims of Christ, as Christian did in Hebrews?

Share your ideas with your study friend.

The Better Way

Christian, our name for the Hebrews author, also had a brilliant mind for logic. To Jews in his day, who relied only on moral law, as my mother did, Christian could prove the validity and truth of Jesus, God's Son. Isn't it remarkable that the Bible can explain a spiritual truth in an earthly way, using logic to help ordinary people think in spiritual terms? Through Christian's words, God not only spoke to Jews of Christian's day but also speaks to people today who need logic to accompany their faith. I hope the words in today's study encourage you, helping you logically piece together what some "churchy" words in Christianity mean.

Christian begins by clearly describing the tabernacle (which we've discussed in previous chapters, but without these details):

> "Now the first covenant had regulations for worship and also an earthly sanctuary. A tabernacle was set up. In its first room were the lampstand, the table and the consecrated bread; this was called the Holy Place. Behind the second curtain was a room called the Most Holy Place, which had the golden altar of incense and the gold-covered ark of the covenant. This ark contained the gold jar of manna, Aaron's staff that had budded, and the stone tablets of the covenant"
>
> (Hebrews 9:1–4).

Tell why you think an image of the ancient place of God's presence is important today.

Lamp for My Path

As these words confirm, the first covenant set up a framework for our worship today. The mobile tabernacle, a symbol of God moving with His people, was always reassembled the same way at the next stop. In the outer courtyard was the Holy Place, containing three items. The first, a lamp-stand, reminds us of an important concept in the Bible: light. Remember, the Israelites of the Old Testament, as well as Christians and Jews in the New Testament, did not have matches, pilot lights, or batteries. If the fire went out, they were in trouble. From the beginning of history, when God said, "Let there be light" (Genesis 1:3), the Jews had depended on God's light. Maybe you can remember the words of Psalm 119:105, from Study 17, or other Scriptures that remind us to rely on light. Take a moment now to rejoice over God's light in your heart.

Write here, as you remember them, words from Scripture that refer to light:

Besides your study friend, with whom can you share these words about the light of Jesus Christ?

Light in My Heart

The Hebrew people had depended on God since the beginning of history, in the Garden of Eden, for light. Since God created *all* light, it's believable that He provided a smaller version, a pillar of fire, to lead them in their exodus through the desert. Even before that, when all Egypt lay in dark-ness during the Passover days, God's Word tells us the Israelites had light in their homes (Exodus 10:23). Centuries later, in the dark pasture lands, as David tended his sheep, and later when he faced dark days of his king-dom, he prayed, "Send forth your light and your truth, let them guide me" (Psalm 43:3). The prophets and patriarchs (righteous fathers) relied on God's light to guide them. Even Job, who had suffered illness and the death of his family, said, "by his light I walked through darkness" (Job 29:3). Jesus said, "I am the light of the world" in John 8:12. He also challenges you: "You are the light of the world. . . . let your light shine before men, that they may see your good deeds and praise your Father in heaven" (Matthew 5:14, 16). Just as God's light never goes out, the light of the lamp in the Holy Place was never to expire. God instructed Moses to keep these lamps burning, tended regularly by Aaron's family, the Levites, for generations (Leviticus 24:1–4).

✤ FRIEND TO FRIEND ✤

As God did with Job and David long ago, how has He walked with you through darkness?

Share with your study friend. Decide ways you both could share your experiences in God's light with others.

The second item in the Holy Place was a table, placed on the north side, opposite the lampstand (Exodus 26:35). God gave His people a recipe for making 12 loaves of bread (Leviticus 24:5–8) and instructions for placing them, along with incense: "Set them in two rows, six in each row, on the table of pure gold before the Lord. . . . This bread is to be set out before the Lord regularly . . . as a lasting covenant." Then He gave instructions for the Levites—and only them—to eat the bread in a holy place and replenish it with new loaves offered by the people. Even when the Hebrew people moved, they kept the showbread on the table, wrapped with the plates (and jars for a drink offering, and other utensils) in a blue cloth, covered with red cloth and then an outer protection of hides to keep it in place. They were faithful to keep the observance as a lasting covenant.

Today we still observe the covenant, using bread and drink offerings in Christian denominations. However, under the new covenant, you observe the bread and wine as Jesus, who gave His offering—His body and blood—as a sacrifice for us. He says, "I am the bread of life. He who comes to me will never go hungry, and he who believes in me will never be thirsty" (John 6:35). He also said, "This is my blood of the new testament, which is shed for many" (Mark 14:24 KJV).

Inside the Holy Place was an entrance into the Most Holy Place. Look back at Hebrews 9:3–4. What two items were there?

As you read Hebrews, you will find two items in the Most Holy Place: the gold altar for incense, and the ark of the covenant containing manna, Aaron's staff, and the Ten Commandments. The manna was actual manna—bread that fell from heaven—which the Israelites had saved since the exodus, probably in a terra cotta jar. Years later Jesus explained why it was important: "Your forefathers ate the manna in the desert, yet they died. But here is the bread that comes down from heaven, which a man may eat and not die. . . . If anyone eats of this bread, he will live forever. This bread is my flesh, which I will give for the life of the world" (John 6:49–51).

What three things were inside the ark?

1.

2.

3.

Write what you've heard about these:

The second item in the ark was Aaron's staff. At one point during the exodus, the people turned against Moses and Aaron. God led Moses to settle the matter by asking 12 men (one from each tribe) to lay down a staff before the Lord, who would bless the staff of the man He chose for leader. In 24 hours Aaron's staff had not only sprouted, but also budded, blossomed, and produced almonds! It was put in the Tent of Meeting to remind future generations of God's life-giving power! [Extra reading: Numbers 17.]

Also in the ark were the Ten Commandments, discussed in previous studies. Portrayed in the awesome decorative gold were angels hovering over the mercy seat (atonement cover). Christian says, "Above the ark were the cherubim of the Glory, overshadowing the atonement cover. But we cannot discuss these things in detail now" (Hebrews 9:5). [For further study of the tabernacle and ark, read *A Woman's Heart: God's Dwelling Place* by Beth Moore.]

❧ FRIEND TO FRIEND ❧

What have you learned about these three items in the ark in this Bible study?

How are these three items symbolic in your life?

Share with your study friend how you once felt and how you now feel about them.

Share with your study friend about your certainty of heaven, living in the Most Holy Place, in the presence of God for eternity.

Shedding of Blood, a Worthy Sacrifice

As Christian reminds us of the differences between priests and the High Priest, which we have studied earlier, he adds one detail: "When everything had been arranged like this, the priests entered regularly into the outer room to carry on their ministry. But only the high priest entered the inner room, and that only once a year, and never without blood, which he offered for himself and for the sins the people had committed in ignorance" (Hebrews 9:6–7). When the priest went into the inner room (the Most Holy Place, or Holy of Holies) once a year, verse 7 says, he never entered *without blood.* What do you think "without blood" signifies?

After considering carefully our study of the priests' duties in this book, write what you think "without blood" means, as it applies to the Old Testament sacrifice.

Explain how you think this applies to Jesus' death in the New Testament:

Because He rose from the dead, how can His resurrection encourage you?

When you were a child, did you ever take a blood oath with a buddy? A friend and I scratched ourselves with a dull piece of tin once, but each of us was afraid to draw blood, so we just touched wrists together and pretended we'd made a blood sacrifice to seal our friendship. The friendship lasted about as long as the scratch. Before long, we'd forgotten our pact to be forever friends. Today's blood—or the lack of it—doesn't seem to seal a pact.

In verses 8–10, Christian explains: "The Holy Spirit was showing by this that the way into the Most Holy Place had not yet been disclosed as long as the first tabernacle was still standing. This is an illustration for the present time, indicating that the gifts and sacrifices being offered were not able to clear the conscience of the worshipper. They are only a matter of food and drink and various ceremonial washings—external regulations applying until the time of the new order."

The time had come for a new order—a new covenant with a living

Lord! Notice these words in verse 8: "the *way* into the Most Holy Place [that is, the presence of God, or heaven] had not yet been disclosed." Exactly what is *the way*?

❧ FRIEND TO FRIEND ❧

According to Hebrews 9:8–10, what do the sacrifices mean under the New Testament?

Who establishes the new order?

In John 14:5, Thomas, one of the disciples, asked Jesus about the way: "'Lord, we don't know where you are going, so how can we know the way?' Jesus answered, 'I am the way and the truth and the life'" (John 14:6). What a wonderful truth: Jesus is the way to heaven, the Most Holy Place. The way to heaven is not a *what* but a *who*! Furthermore, we saw in Study 13 that He was the way of access through the curtain separating the Holy Place from the Most Holy Place! He's the one and only thread weaving between, connecting the two. He destroyed all barriers between you and heaven when His body was broken for you. Hallelujah! He takes you right through to a place of spiritual intimacy with God.

❧ FRIEND TO FRIEND ❧

Are there times you long for the Most Holy Place with Jesus, but can't seem to find its peace and spiritual intimacy?

Discuss with your study friend how to find the way to the Most Holy Place.

My logical brain is satisfied that Hebrews is Truth with a capital *T*. My feeling heart also sees Truth in the Most Holy Place. I long for that home, in the safety of my high priest. Am I there all the time? No, but I long for that intimacy all the time.

When I think of the Most Holy Place with my heart and not my brain, I *know* that's where Jesus is, where the intimacy with His Presence is. I don't want surface worship or external regulations. I want the real thing: life everlasting with Almighty God!

The Old Testament is your heritage. The model of the high priest helps you understand the need for a Savior willing to shed His blood for you. He's the Bread of heaven, He's the Light, He's the Curtain—the Way, He's the Lamb sacrificed and broken for you. In short, He's your everything! As you study His Word and pray, you'll find Him as your Way to the Most Holy Place.

Touch My Heart, Lord Jesus
Bread of Heaven, take me into the Most Holy Place with You. Consecrate me, Lord, so I may be pure. Help me to understand with my heart, not just with my mind, deeper truth and love. Prepare the full banquet for me, O Holy One. Light my way to spiritual understanding and the highest love as I follow Your way. Amen.

STUDY 20 *My Heritage: Clean and Ransomed*
HEBREWS 9:11–22

IN 1980 after my husband died suddenly, I had to go to our county's probate judge and make sure our family had taken care of all the details—and what overwhelming details they were! My father went with me for the first visit, then my son and daughter—and sometimes my father, mother, and children all crowded in the probate judge's office, to take care of details. One of the most important things I had to provide for the records (and pay for) was an "original" death certificate (not copied). The probate judge filed several "original" copies, my attorney filed one, the funeral home requested two. Each insurance company needed one, and I produced three for the sale of a tractor to the buyer, the bank, and the tractor company, adding a few more "originals" when I sold my husband's old farm pickup. I gave one each to the city, county, and federal tax offices! Death certificates were flying like falling leaves out of my pockets, as the inheritance money dwindled! No legal transaction could be made without a will and a death certificate—our proof of death.

Our Holy Inheritance
In today's study, we find how today's wills and death certificates compare with proof of death in Jesus' day. Translated from Greek into modern English, the language in this study is beautiful prose. Christian is on a roll! Can you hear his words moving faster and faster as he says, "When Christ came as high priest of the good things that are already here, he went through the greater and more perfect tabernacle that is not man-made, that is to say,

not a part of this creation" (Hebrews 9:11). If the tabernacle set a precedent of good things, Jesus provided better. If the Most Holy Place was holy, then heaven was holier! Priests entered the first; the Son of God entered the second! Jesus, in one mighty surge of energy at the resurrection moment, burst forth from the tomb and left it empty! Earthly, temporal sacrifices were exchanged for heavenly, eternal redemption when He broke through!

Christian explains:

> "He did not enter by means of the blood of goats and calves; but he entered the Most Holy Place once for all by his own blood, having obtained eternal redemption. The blood of goats and bulls and the ashes of a heifer sprinkled on those who are ceremonially unclean sanctify them so that they are out-wardly clean. How much more, then, will the blood of Christ, who through the eternal Spirit offered himself unblemished to God, cleanse our consciences from acts that lead to death, so that we may serve the living God!"   (Hebrews 9:12–14).

What do you think "once for all" means? In Study 21 you will find more about this phrase. Remember it for future reference.

❧ FRIEND TO FRIEND ❧

Find in Hebrews 9:12–14 the words, "How much more . . . will Christ . . . cleanse our consciences." Pray and give thanks for the sacrifice of the Unblemished One. Write your prayer here.

Why does verse 14 say we are cleansed?

Share with your study friend.

Can you imagine the primitive ritual of sprinkling the blood of goats and bulls and, after burning a heifer, taking the ashes and sprinkling them on an unclean person to clean them? It sounds impossible, doesn't it? You'd think those ashes and blood would make someone dirty, instead of clean, wouldn't you? Now think on this for a moment: what ingredients do you need for homemade soap? If you grew up as a baby boomer, you may remember Granny on *The Beverly Hillbillies* making lye soap. My grandmother also made homemade soap from lye (an acid) and lard (animal fat). When the two are combined through heat (fire), soap forms on the top of the mixture, which can be cut into squares and used to cleanse the skin. Ashes from an altar are similar to lye. It's easy to see that the animal fat from the fire, mixing with the ashes and washing down the hill to a river, would provide a few soapsuds for women washing clothes on the rocks at the shoals below. Maybe the laundry ritual became a learning experience for the religious ritual. Soap not only cleans but kills germs, preventing infection and illness. When I think of the elements of sacrifice being the ingredients for soap, then I can understand a simple principle of cleansing.

Hebrews talks about Christ being *unblemished*. That word leads me to recall one day when I taught a group of slow learners a vocabulary lesson for these words: *spy, spot, sport,* and *spout*. One little boy read a sentence using a synonym for one of our words. (The rest of the class was to guess the word.) He read loudly, "Looking for Maria, Jerry turned the corner and blemished her." The class scratched their heads. No one knew the word. I couldn't think of it either. He explained: "I looked it up in a dictionary. Don't *blemish* mean *spot?*"

"Doesn't," I corrected.

"Well, don't it or doesn't it?" he asked again.

"Yes," I said. "A blemish can be a spot."

"Well, my sentence means: Looking for Maria, Jerry turned the corner and spotted her. She was standing right there on the sidewalk!"

I left school teaching the next year. (But I have wondered what that student is doing today.)

Sometimes we don't understand the difference between blemished and unblemished. Most of the time, however, we just don't care.

To Serve the Living God

"For this reason Christ is the mediator of a new covenant, that those who are called may receive the promised eternal inheritance—now that he has died as a ransom to set them free from the sins committed under the first covenant" (Hebrews 9:15). Christ Jesus paid the ransom; but he did more than that. He *was* the ransom! He *became* the price, the cost of your freedom! Christ is a ransom to set us free from sins committed under the first covenant. Wow! Christian gives an example of what he means: "In the case of a will, it is necessary to prove the death of the one who made it" (Hebrews 9:16). [Press the pause button: It's the law! It requires the evidence of blood—proof of death to make a clean settlement; a death certificate to sanctify/validate the will.] Now finish the Hebrews passage: "because a will is in force only when somebody has died; it never takes effect while the one who made it is living. This is why even the first covenant was not put into effect without blood. When Moses had proclaimed every commandment of the law to all the people, he took the blood of calves, together with water, scarlet wool and branches of hyssop, and sprinkled the scroll and all the people" (Hebrews 9:17–19).

Moses said, "'This is the blood of the covenant, which God has commanded you to keep.' In the same way, he sprinkled with the blood both the tabernacle and everything used in its ceremonies. In fact, the law requires that nearly everything be cleansed with blood, and without the shedding of blood there is no forgiveness" (Hebrews 9:20–22). This is an important concept, not only for Christian but also for you. Even in the secular world, the law still occasionally requires DNA from a suspect's blood to prove who is guilty, who is released, and who makes retribution for sins by going to jail.

Touch My Heart, Lord Jesus

Lamb of God, I don't understand all about the sacrifice You made . . . how You could pay the price for my ransom and be the ransom at the same time. Because of my ignorance, as Hebrews says, forgive me. Help me to accept Your perfect love and to understand that without the shedding of blood there is no forgiveness. May I serve You as one forgiven! Amen.

UNIT 5 *My Sacrifice of Faith*

GODLY WOMAN, look with anticipation as you approach the next five studies. Here are a few how-to principles we'll explore in Unit 5: how to welcome Jesus as the overseer of your soul, how to avoid worry as you stand and wait, how to blaze a new trail in your spiritual walk, how to live the good life, how to draw near to God in full assurance of faith, how to remain faithful in your Bible study/church attendance, how to face suffering, and how to build your life on a firm foundation. We will end the unit with a survey of faith down through the ages—the Bible in a nutshell.

In this unit, you can fine-tune your faith. Christian will take us back to some of the earlier Scriptures you've studied in Hebrews and fill in the details. Catch the spirit of movement as you study! You're on a roll now. Start the study and move out!

STUDY 21 *My Once-and-for-All Sacrifice*
HEBREWS 9:23–28

I'll never forget "Miss Nancy" Owens, my third-grade teacher. She encouraged us, but she ran a tight ship. She *commanded*—not *demanded*—respect from her students. One day she wrote names on the board for talking. Having no recess and two afterschool detentions were a fate worse than death in the third grade! A friend asked me a question and I said, "Shh!" Miss Nancy heard me and wrote both of our names on the board. I tried to explain, but Miss Nancy had made up her mind.

Then the unbelievable happened. At the end of the class, Miss Nancy picked up her eraser, and with a magnificent double swoop, erased all our names. Turning, she said, "Don't ever say I did nothing for you." After school that day, we vowed we'd always remember Miss Nancy's forgiving swoop.

His Forgiving Heart

Today's study describes in detail how Jesus brought forgiveness in one fell swoop. One moment in history offered mercy to you, overflowing from a forgiving heart. Hebrews 9:15 (Study 20) gave you the promise of forgiveness as your inheritance: "those who are called may receive the promised eternal inheritance." To be sure the Hebrews understood, Christian (our name for the writer) compared sacrifices under the law to Jesus' sacrifice: "It was necessary, then, for the copies of the heavenly things to be purified with these sacrifices, but the heavenly things themselves with better sacrifices than these" (Hebrews 9:23). Just as correction fluid covers mistakes we make on paper, so Jesus is able to white-out (or blot out) our wrongdoing. The law was just a copy, with spots of imperfection. Remember this verse from Hebrews 8:5? "They [Levitical priests] serve at a sanctuary that is a copy and shadow of what is in heaven." Jesus, the original Master, has the power to wipe clean the blemishes and dark spots.

Christian says: "For Christ did not enter a man-made sanctuary that was only a copy of the true one; he entered heaven itself, now to appear for us in God's presence. Nor did he enter heaven to offer himself again and again, the way the high priest enters the Most Holy Place every year with blood that is not his own. Then Christ would have had to suffer many times since the creation of the world. But now he has appeared once for all at the end of the ages to do away with sin by the sacrifice of himself" (Hebrews 9:24–26). He destroyed sin in one fell swoop!

In Hebrews 9:24–26, what did Jesus *not* do?

What *did* He do?

Why did He enter heaven?

For whom did he appear as advocate before His Father?

How often did He enter?

Why did He appear for you?

Which blood sacrifice did He bring?

❧ FRIEND TO FRIEND ❧

Share your feelings about Jesus, your advocate, with your study friend.

Jesus didn't enter an earthly sanctuary, made by humans, but entered heaven, to appear before God Himself as your advocate. Notice the word *us* in verse 24. He did this for you. In one fell swoop Jesus, entering heaven—with His own blood—broke through the veil (or curtain), once for all, to do away with your sin. Christian says "now . . . at the end of the ages" (v. 26), indicating the New Testament view that they were living in the last days. So are we, still in the Christian church era. However, no matter when the last day of the "end of the ages" comes, Jesus died only once: once for all ages, One for all people.

No Recycling for Me

The incarnate Christ died only once; we will do the same: "Just as man is destined to die once, and after that to face judgment" (Hebrews 9:27). This short clause includes two important truths. First, reincarnation is not possible. You are destined to die only once, not to be recycled as a cat, a king, or a holy cow!

Second, all of us will face judgment. Because God is just, He must bring justice. You would not think much of a god who allowed chaos and never brought justice.

In twenty-first-century America, people live as if there is no judgment, but you can be sure that in eternity God will take all the time necessary to review all your sins. You cannot avoid that judgment. However, here's good news: just as you'll die only once—and will be judged only once—"so Christ was sacrificed once to take away the sins of many people; and he will appear a second time, not to bear sin, but to bring salvation to those who are waiting for him" (Hebrews 9:28).

Here's another place in God's Word for a big hallelujah! Will you have to stand quaking in your boots, afraid of eternal damnation in a fiery hell? No. You can draw near to the throne in full assurance of faith (Hebrews 10:22). You don't have to grovel before a mean despot God. As a Christian, you bow before Him, yes, but out of a grateful heart, because He loves you. You voluntarily sit at His feet to worship Him and learn from Him. Lift your chin. Raise your eyes. You can be confident! Your loving God desires a personal relationship with you. You don't have any frailties, weaknesses, meanness, or sin that can make Him despise you.

When you get to heaven, you can say you trust Jesus to bring you to salvation, and in one fell swoop, you, too, will enter.

According to Hebrews 9, how should you feel about death and judgment?

How confidently do you live your life every day?

No Worry for Me

Paul says, "Rejoice in the Lord always. . . . Do not be anxious about anything" (Philippians 4:4, 6). As a woman who is confident in Jesus, you do not have to worry as you wait. Look back at Hebrews 9:28. To whom will Jesus appear, to bring salvation? Titus 2:13–14 confirms that part of the Christian life is *waiting*: "While we wait for the blessed hope—the glorious appearing of our great God and Savior, Jesus Christ, who gave himself for us to redeem us . . . and to purify for himself a people that are his very own." Waiting for God to act, waiting for rewards for good behavior, waiting for prayers to be answered—waiting is the hardest part of the Christian life. Yet Hebrews 9:28 is clear: He will appear a second time to bring salvation *to those who are waiting for Him.* He's your assurance.

You may be waiting now for an answer to an urgent concern. Never fear. God will answer. He always teaches you in the waiting. As you wait, remember these verses:

"And when I was burdened with worries, you comforted me and made me feel secure" (Psalm 94:19 CEV).

"He may not get up and give you the bread, just because you are his friend. But he will get up and give you as much as you need, simply because you are not ashamed to keep on asking" (Luke 11:8 CEV).

"And my God will meet all your needs according to his glorious riches in Christ Jesus." (Philippians 4:19)

What things do you do or say that indicate you are confident?

Have you ever been sin-sick (sick of a sin that keeps enticing you)? What happened?

As you feel comfortable to do so, share with your study friend.

Waiting with Assurance

Jesus' disciples were waiting, lingering after He had just ascended into heaven, when angels told them: "Men of Galilee . . . why do you stand here looking into the sky? This same Jesus, who has been taken from you into heaven, will come back in the same way you have seen him go into heaven" (Acts 1:11). You have assurance that Christ will reappear during the second coming, at the end of the age; but you also have assurance that He comes to you at the time of your salvation experience with Him, and His Holy Spirit lives within you daily. He is the overseer of your soul (1 Peter 2:25), standing by you daily, enabling you to live with assurance.

❧ FRIEND TO FRIEND ❧

Share with your study friend the words that encourage you in a time of wait and worry.

How do you allow Jesus to be the "overseer of your soul" during hard times?

Touch My Heart, Lord Jesus
Overseer of my soul, thank You for dying for me. I am so grateful for that moment in history that overcame sin in one swoop. But Lord, I'm even more grateful for Your Holy Spirit, who assures me of that salvation every day. Thank You for giving me confidence as I wait. I dare to look forward to heaven, without worry, because of Your love. Amen.

STUDY 22 *I'll Be Perfect Forever!*

HEBREWS 10:1–18

Hebrews 10
The old-time law said flesh should burn,
But never was our Father pleased.
He gave His Son, who did not spurn
The cross, with sin and all disease.

Now enemies fall at His feet,
And they've become a footstool, blind;
But Christians now God's law repeat
He writes it in their heart and mind.
For we go in the Holy Place,
Go down a new and living trail!
We enter Jesus' holy space;
See! Christ's own body is the veil!

So let us draw near unto Him,
In full assurance of faith, not fight.
Let's meet together, not grow dim,
And spur one another to do right.

—EDNA M. ELLISON, © 2002

On my first date, I had a horrible time. My boyfriend appeared without a car to walk me to the movies. (I had assumed his father or brother would drive us; the shoes that matched my outfit were not comfortable for walking.) The night was dark, my feet were hurting, and the movie was mediocre. On the way home, he put his arm around my shoulder as we walked along. His stride was twice as long as mine, and his gait became a handicap as his arm bounced back and forth on the back of my neck—when he stepped right, I stepped left (or left, right, left!). As we awkwardly rounded one corner, I saw a shadow behind a large tree. I hesitated, and his long legs walked on, his arm knocking my just-placed hair straight up over my head! Peeking out from the hair in my eyes, I saw arms move from behind the tree! Instantly I screamed, and my boyfriend stopped walking. When I showed him the dark shadow, he saw it, too: definitely a monster hoodlum looming over the sidewalk, ready to beat us up! He grabbed a big stick and slowly approached the tree, with me four feet behind him. Behind the tree, he found a smaller tree with soft limbs waving in the breeze. I had seen the shadow of the small tree behind the big tree, not a robber or a monster, after all. (By the way, I never went out with the loping boyfriend again.)

❧ FRIEND TO FRIEND ❧

Did you ever have a scary experience with a shadow? What happened?

Share with your study friend.

Today's study discusses shadows—not a spooky tree or a monster in your imagination, but the shadow of a perfect pattern. We learn in the first few verses below that shadows are not perfect representations. No matter how near they get to perfection, they are not perfect.

> "The law is only a shadow of the good things that are coming—not the realities themselves. For this reason it can never, by the same sacrifices repeated endlessly year after year, make perfect those who draw near to worship. If it could, would they not have stopped being offered? For the worshippers would have been cleansed once for all, and would no longer have felt guilty for their sins. But those sacrifices are an annual reminder of sins, because it is impossible for the blood of bulls and goats to take away sins. Therefore, when Christ came into the world, he said: 'Sacrifice and offering you did not desire, but a body you prepared for me; with burnt offerings and sin offerings you were not pleased. Then I said, "Here I am—it is written about me in the scroll—I have come to do your will, O God."'"
> —Hebrews 10:1–7

Christian reviews what you have already learned about the insufficiency of the animal sacrifices compared to the sufficient sacrifice of Jesus. He quotes Psalm 40:6–8, noting God's dissatisfaction with burnt offerings and religious rites without sincerity or faith. The end of Psalm 40:8 continues after "I desire to do your will, O my God" with these words: "your law is within my heart."

You may say, "Now, tell me again why God gave the laws, for Moses to write in stone, in the first place?" My best answer is, "Because they were noteworthy." If you want something remembered, you write it down. Journalists say that if you want to be remembered in history, you must

(1) write something to be preserved or (2) do something important enough for someone else to record and preserve. Then generations will remember what was done or written. According to Hebrews 10:3, the Levitical laws were an "annual reminder" of sins. They were important, yes, but only as a shadow of good things to come (Hebrews 10:1).

A Two-Verse Synopsis

In his own logical way, Christian summarizes what he's quoted from Psalm 40 as a dichotomy (two parts): "First he said, 'Sacrifices and offerings, burnt offerings and sin offerings you did not desire, nor were you pleased with them' (although the law required them to be made). Then he said, 'Here I am, I have come to do your will.' He sets aside the first to establish the second" (Hebrews 10:8–9). Jesus is the ultimate fulfillment of the Old Testament, including the Psalms. When He came to do God's will, God set aside the old laws. How do you know you are doing God's will? Explore ideas in this activity. Circle the items below that give you clues that you are following God's will:

✎ Verses in the Bible

✎ Shakespeare's writings or other words of wisdom trusted by the world

✎ Prayer

✎ Self-help programs on television

✎ Meditation on words from a sermon, devotional, or other Christian writings I trust

✎ My fairy godmother

✎ A sense of the Holy Spirit

❧ FRIEND TO FRIEND ❧

Share your answers with your study friend.

How did you do in the activity above? I'm sure you found that every other item would be helpful: Bible reading, prayer, meditation on wisdom you've received from other trusted Christians, and direct revelation from the Holy

Spirit can nudge you in the direction of God's will for your life. Absorb God's Word—this is the most important principle of successful Christian living. Read other Christian commentaries on Christian living, and spend time in prayer. Remember, don't substitute the good for the best. The best thing you can do to understand God's will is to read what He says.

Christian gives us an uplifting message in the next verses. Pause and think of each phrase: "And by that will, we have been made holy [How?] through the sacrifice of the body of Jesus Christ [How often?] once [For whom?] for all. [Who has a boring job?] Day after day every priest stands and performs his religious duties; again and again he offers the same sacrifices, [Which kind?] which can never take away sins. But when this priest [Jesus] had offered [When?] for all time [Offered what?] one sacrifice for sins, he sat down [Where?] at the right hand of God" (Hebrews 10:10–12).

Same Ol', Same Ol'

Do you ever use the expression "same ol', same ol'"? This describes the Levitical priests' rituals. Without faith, and without the Holy Spirit's help, your religion can become ritual, too. Sunday church attendance can become mere ceremony. However, you can change that: you can worship God, pray for your pastor as he preaches, and take notes on his sermon and the choir anthem for later meditation. You can sing choruses and welcome the Holy Spirit into your heart as you'd welcome a visitor to your church!

The same ol', same ol' in your life can be as ineffective as that of the priests Christian describes. But then he points out something new: this priest, after offering an effective sacrifice, sat at the right (righteous, prestigious) hand of God! He blazed a new trail to set people on the right path! He could sit down satisfied because He had satisfied the requirements. Christian says, "Since that time he waits for his enemies to be made his footstool, because by one sacrifice he has made perfect forever those who are being made holy" (Hebrews 10:13–14). God also says this to the church at Philadelphia: "those who are of the synagogue of Satan, who . . . are liars— I will make them come and fall down at your feet and acknowledge that I have loved you" (Revelation 3:9). What a satisfaction! Be patient, dear godly woman, in the wait, God is perfecting you!

Hebrews 10:15–18 reviews Hebrews 8:10 (Study 17): "The Holy Spirit also testifies to us about this. First he says: 'This is the covenant I will make with them after that time, says the Lord. I will put my laws in their hearts, and I will write them on their minds'" (Hebrews 10:15–16). In Hebrews 10:16, to which time does the Holy Spirit point when He says "after that time"? After the most momentous time in history, when Jesus offered for all time a sacrifice for your sins, a new time began. All things in the past (old covenants, repeated rituals, bloody sacrifices) were obsolete.

Christian goes on, "'Their sins and lawless acts I will remember no more.' And where these have been forgiven, there is no longer any sacrifice for sin" (Hebrews 10:17–18). Once you have been forgiven, you don't need to sacrifice. Remember, there is no condemnation in Christ. As surely as He sits at the right hand of God in heaven, is Holy Spirit whispers His Word in your heart. And as He whispers, He sanctifies (makes you more perfect) until you follow His path all the way to heaven, where you'll be perfect forever!

❧ FRIEND TO FRIEND ❧

Are you ever dissatisfied with your church?

. . . with your pastor?

. . . with your church choir or worship team?

. . . with someone else's attitude at church?

How can you blaze a new trail to get your worship experiences on a better path? How can your focus on Jesus and heaven's throne?

Using Hebrews 10:12–15, write where you think God is:

Where is Jesus?

Where is the Holy Spirit?

Discuss with your study friend.

Touch My Heart, Lord Jesus
Jesus, thank You for being the unblemished Lamb who takes away the sins of the world. May I always be grateful, O Lord and sanctifier, that You

suffered to make me holy—sinless before God! Help me start something new in my life and my church. I know I can find satisfaction and contentment in You, O great Satisfier! Amen.

STUDY 23 *I'm Living the Good Life*
HEBREWS 10:19–39

IN 1996 I spent a night in London with a very handsome medical doctor, his beautiful red-haired wife, and their adorable, intelligent son—who were leaving a luxurious life in a mansion to go to a dangerous area of the Middle East. That night, university students who came for a party shared photos of their Christian fathers, mothers, sisters, brothers, and cousins who had been murdered for their faith. When I asked them about their future, they said, "Oh, we live the good life! All of us will go back home (to the Middle East) soon, where we'll live an even better life—the best life—where we can share the hope of Jesus with those who killed our loved ones. We can't wait to get there!" I'll never forget their eyes, filled with joy and hope.

At the very moment you are reading this, Christians are dying for their faith around the world—just as Christians were being persecuted in the days when the Hebrew letter circulated. Most of them are courageous because they know—even in suffering—they are living the good life!

The Book of Hebrews starts many chapters and sections with "Therefore . . ." (2:1; 3:1; 4:1; 4:14; 6:1; 10:19; 12:1; 12:12; and 12:28). Christian, our name for the writer of Hebrews, uses logic to hook one section to another, just as he builds the verses in this study on those in Study 22. He implies, "Since everything I've said so far is true—can you check *all the above* for what I said just before this?—then see if what I'm about to say makes sense! Work with me, now, buddy. God's doing a new thing with us! The sky's the limit with our generation!" Listen with your heart as you hear the first section of Christian's next logical sentence: "Therefore, brothers, since we have confidence to enter the Most Holy Place by the blood of Jesus." (Hebrews 10:19). Like the students in London, you can live a life of confidence to enter the Most Holy Place—heaven—but you can also have confidence to live a vigorous Christian life on earth.

❧ FRIEND TO FRIEND ❧

Have you ever spent time with anyone whose families have been martyrs for Christ? What did they say?

Do you know people who suffer for the cause of Christ today? (Clergy or laypersons) Describe the situation:

I'm Living the Good Life!

How do you get on this new trail to the new life? "By a new and living way opened for us through the curtain, that is, his body" (Hebrews 10:20). Dwelling inside your heart is the Holy Spirit of Jesus, who opens the way to heaven through His broken body. Life through the curtain (His body) is incredible to most folks, yet you can:

live through the life of Jesus,
see through the eyes of Jesus,
hear with the ears of Jesus,
love through the heart of Jesus,
have the faith of Jesus, and
live the righteousness of Jesus as you follow His example.

❧ FRIEND TO FRIEND ❧

∴

What do you think the mathematical sign (∴) above means?

You probably do know of suffering among God's people, therefore (∴), what can you do to help?

Discuss your answers with your study friend.

I'm Living the High Life!

As you allow Him to live through you, you catch glimpses of heaven through the veil, which you were unable to see before. The closer you lean to Him, the more reality you can see. Sometimes in my church, we sing, "I can feel the brush of angel's wings... the presence of the Lord is in this place." In his book *Angels: God's Secret Agents*, Billy Graham says, "I've never seen an angel ... [but] I believe in angels because I have sensed their presence in my life on special occasions."

Draw Near to God in Full Assurance of Faith

Christian adds, "and since we have a great priest (our Overseer) over the house of God" (Hebrews 10:21). Stop and look back over the last few verses in Hebrews. Since we have confidence to enter heaven—through Jesus, who opened a new path through the veil, or curtain—and since He's my high priest, living within me, then we have assurance: ". . . let us draw near to God with a sincere heart in full assurance of faith, having our hearts sprinkled to cleanse us from a guilty conscience and having our bodies washed with pure water" (Hebrews 10:22).

For years this was my son's, Jack's, favorite verse. It was so elaborate I couldn't memorize it, but it was so beautiful I wanted to try. I am grateful to God that Jack patiently taught me this verse. I'd ask him often to quote it, and I finally have it in my brain! First, you draw near to Him, in the shadow of His wings: "He will cover you with his feathers, and under his wings you will find refuge" (Psalm 91:4). Second, you have a sincere heart. Third, you have full assurance: "I sing in the shadow of your wings" (Psalm 63:7). Fourth, your assurance comes from faith: *Forsaking All I Trust Him*. Then He gives you (1) a clean conscience—inside, and (2) a clean body—outside! Only Jesus can do that.

❧ FRIEND TO FRIEND ❧

Spend a moment meditating over God's blessings in your life. Open your hand. Pray with your study friend for blessings God has placed in your hand. Then look closely at Hebrews 10:23 and answer these questions:

How do you hold?

To what do you hold?

Which hope do you hold?

Why do you hold?

A few years ago we invited into our home for dinner a teenager whom the police had found in a road lying on the middle yellow line. When they found him he was high on drugs and he wore no shirt or underwear, just a pair of jeans. His hair hung down to his shoulders, matted and dirty. The night he ate with us, he wore the new clothes my husband had bought. His hair was neatly tied in a ponytail. Before long, I listened as he gave his testimony at a small-group Bible study. I hardly recognized him. He was dressed in first-class casual clothes. His hair was neatly cropped around his ears. He quoted Hebrews 10:22. God had cleaned him up inside and out!

God says, "He gathers the lambs in his arms and carries them close to his heart" (Isaiah 40:11).

As Jesus holds us in His arms, "Let us hold [How?] unswervingly [To what?] to the hope [Which hope? The hope. . .] we profess, [Why?] for he who promised is faithful" (Hebrews 10:23). As we learned in Study 10, be passionate as you declare your hope! Almighty God is faithful. You can trust Him to come through for you. Your hope means *Holding On to Promises Eternal*. You can do it! You can hold on to the solid hope!

In Fact, I'm Living the Better Life

Christian says, "And let us consider how we may spur one another on toward love and good deeds" (Hebrews 10:24).

The early Christians were under persecution, just as many Christians experience it today in some countries. Yet they continued to love even their enemies and to do good deeds even in prison or other places where they faced death. For example, Christian says, "Let us not give up meeting together, as some are in the habit of doing, but let us encourage one another—and all the more as you see the Day approaching" (Hebrews 10:25). I hope you hear the urgent tone in the first phrase. Meeting is a habit. If you are out of the habit of meeting together with a church fellowship, don't let any time factor, grouchy person, or your own sagging spirit stop you from uniting with God's people. In the long run, they'll encourage you as much as you encourage them! Now look at the last phrase. Do you hear an even more urgent tone? If today were the last day on earth, what would you be doing now?

As Christian follows his own advice in verse 25, do you get it? Is he spurring you on?

⚜ FRIEND TO FRIEND ⚜

Toward what two goals does Christian say you can spurs others on?

1.

2.

By the side of each number above, write one thing you can do with your family or friends to spur them on in these two areas.

Share with your study friend.

List some habits you have formed that don't encourage others or yourself:

Share with your study friend. Discuss how you can replace a bad habit with a good one.

A Last-Day Warning

Christian advises: "If we deliberately keep on sinning after we have received the knowledge of the truth, no sacrifice for sins is left, but only a fearful expectation of judgment and of raging fire that will consume the enemies of God" (Hebrews 10:26–27).

God says, "For the wages of sin is death"(Romans 6:23). In other words, sin earns you death in hell, apart from the goodness and mercy of God. Christian reminds you of the law in Deuteronomy 17:6–7: "Anyone who rejected the law of Moses died without mercy on the testimony of two or three witnesses" (Hebrews 10:28). Verses 29–31 warn you about the punishment of rejecting Jesus: "How much more severely do you think a man deserves to be punished who has trampled the Son of God under foot, who has treated as an unholy thing the blood of the covenant that sanctified him, and who has insulted the Spirit of grace? For we know him who said, 'It is mine to avenge; I will repay,' and again, 'The Lord will judge his people.' It is a dreadful thing to fall into the hands of the living God."

Gaining Better Possessions

Christian then helps you to see both sides of the Christian picture (good and bad):

> "Remember those earlier days after you had received the light, when you stood your ground in a great contest in the face of suffering. Sometimes you were publicly exposed to insult and persecution; at other times you stood side by side with those who were so treated. You sympathized with those in prison and joyfully accepted the confiscation of your property, because you knew that you yourselves had better and lasting possessions. So do not throw away your confidence; it will be richly rewarded."
> —Hebrews 10:32–35

Read Hebrews 10:32–34 and make a list of difficult challenges and better possessions that come with being a Christian. Share with your study friend.

Here are difficult challenges you may face as a Christian in verses 32–35. I may have to:

❧ stand my ground in a contest with non-Christians (it may be a shouting contest, or rivalry over my children or over a job)

❧ stand my ground in a contest for what is right among Christians (maybe even in church).

❧ face great suffering

❧ be publicly exposed to insult and persecution

❧ stand up for someone else who is insulted and persecuted

❧ face prison for my faith

❧ sympathize with others in prison

❧ submit to having my property confiscated

Here are better possessions that can motivate you to endure the difficult challenges. I am able to:

❧ remember the early days when I first became a Christian

❧ receive the light of Christ

❧ stand in the face of persecution

❧ reach out to others who suffer

❧ know I'm not alone

❧ stand shoulder to shoulder with other Christians

❧ have a heart of sympathy

❧ be joyful, even without any material possessions

❧ recognize that I have better, eternal possessions than ones on earth

❧ have confidence

❧ trust that my confidence in Jesus will be rewarded

An important word in Hebrews 10:32–35 is *confidence*. Dear reader, no matter what your circumstances this day, keep your confidence. It's worth something. You can trust Him. Your hope and confidence will be rewarded, not in a miserly way, but with the full outpouring of riches from your Lord!

I'm Living a Life of Faith

At times in your life you may wonder why you "keep on keeping on" as a Christian. Dishonest people all around you seem to prosper. Your own family seems to suffer. Maybe you are undergoing great suffering. No matter how hard you try, you seem to fail at many things. Let's face it: it's hard to live a life of faith. Sometimes you won't feel like persevering; you may not want to do God's will. Christian says, "You need to persevere so that when you have done the will of God, you will receive what he has promised. For in just a very little while, 'He who is coming will come and will not delay' " (Hebrews 10:36–37).

Stop and ask questions as you move through the next verse: "But [Who?] my righteous one [What?] will live [How?] by faith. And [What if?] if he shrinks back, I will not be pleased [With whom] with him [or her]" (Hebrews 10:38). Remember, you live by faith. Each of us is given the same measure. How you develop yours is up to you. (Extra reading about righteousness: Habakkuk 2:3–4; Romans 1:17, 3:21–22; Galatians 3:11–14. If you are a Gentile, not a Jew, you may want to pay special attention to the Galatians Scripture.)

Can you say, as Christian says, "But we are not of those who shrink back and are destroyed, but of those who believe and are saved" (Hebrews 10:39)?

❧ FRIEND TO FRIEND ❧

Why do you "keep on keeping on" in your Christian faith?

Why do you do what God does, using His perfect example for your imperfect life?

What must you do to receive His promises?

Who is it that is coming?

When he comes, what will you receive?

Discuss with your study friend what promises God has given you.

Touch My Heart, Lord Jesus
Faithful protector, thank You for holding me close to Your heart. Lord, I dare to draw near You in full assurance of faith! Clean my conscience from guilt;

wash my body with pure water. Help me live like You, O faithful promiser. May I find ways to develop my faith daily. Keep me from evil, Lord, and pour out Your love and promises. Amen.

STUDY 24 *Better Faith, a Definition*
HEBREWS 11:1–22

Hebrews 11
For we know faith is substance pure
Of things we hope and trust will be,
And faith is evidence, we're sure,
Of heav'nly things we cannot see.

By faith the world at God's command
Did form deep seas and mountains tall!
By faith the ark good Noah planned;
By faith did Abram hear the call.

By faith was Rahab saved one day;
By faith strong Jericho would fall;
By faith would baby Moses stay
At Pharaoh's house, to lead them all.

By faith the brave-heart martyrs died;
By faith the bravest hero lives.
By faith we find a better side
Of life to serve Him who forgives.

—EDNA M. ELLISON, © 2002

✤ FRIEND TO FRIEND ✤

As you read Hebrews 11:1–22, list each faithful person. Then write the action each one took by faith. When you complete the list, examine how varied the examples are and share with your study friend how you can use their examples to develop your faith.

When we ended Study 23, our Scripture pointed us to faith: "The righteous will live by faith!" Now, at last, we come to the most lyrical passage in Hebrews. Christian, our name for the writer, must have been a God-inspired poet; his ordinary prose puts my poetry to shame! He says, "Now faith is being sure of what we hope for and certain of what we do not see" (Hebrews 11:1). When I was a child, I memorized the verse like this: "Now faith is the *substance* of things hoped for, the *evidence* of things not seen" (KJV). Substance and evidence are two tangible items. In a court of law, there are two ways to prove guilt or innocence: (1) evidence, such as a testimony which gives proof of a motive, or the opportunity of time and place of the crime; police records of a dead body and a murder weapon; or a written confession; and (2) incriminating substances, such as DNA tests proving blood or hair from the accused was left at the crime scene. Substance backs up evidence.

The two together combine to "tell it like it is." They draw a picture of reality, portraying truth. Two other words in verse 1 set a theme for this chapter: faith and hope. Christian says, "This is what the ancients were commended for" (Hebrews 11:2). Then he lists every faithful ancient person he can think of. We honor these people even today as giants of faith.

> "By faith we understand that the universe was formed at God's command, so that what is seen was not made out of what was visible. By faith Abel offered God a better sacrifice than Cain did. By faith he was commended as a righteous man, when God spoke well of his offerings. And by faith he still speaks, even though he is dead. By faith Enoch was taken from this life, so that he did not experience death; he could not be found, because God had taken him away. For before he was taken, he was commended as one who pleased God."
>
> —Hebrews 11:3–5

A Heritage, Now Yours

After verse 5, Christian pauses to explain in verse 6: "And without faith it is impossible to please God, because anyone who comes to him must believe that he exists and that he rewards those who earnestly seek him." What a great verse! I have trusted Hebrews 11:6 for years. In the hard times, when I struggle to keep my faith strong, I trust that God will reward those who earnestly seek Him. How about you? Are you earnestly seeking Him today? Do you believe by faith that God exists—and that His rewards are real?

Looking Forward

We find another set of people in the next few verses: "By faith Noah, when warned about things not yet seen, in holy fear built an ark to save his family. By his faith he condemned the world and became heir of the righteousness that comes by faith. By faith Abraham, when called to go to a place he would later receive as his inheritance, obeyed and went, even though he did not know where he was going. By faith he made his home in the promised land like a stranger in a foreign country; he lived in tents, as did Isaac and Jacob, who were heirs with him of the same promise. For he was looking forward to the city with foundations, whose architect and builder is God" (Hebrews 11:7–10).

✜ FRIEND TO FRIEND ✜

In Hebrews 11:10, what are they looking for?

As a woman of faith, are you looking forward to heaven? Why or why not?

Name a time you had to move. What were your fears?

Christian says Noah became an heir of righteousness that comes by faith. No doubt he and Abraham both were looking forward, not backward to life as it used to be. They courageously approached the future, leaving their old trappings behind.

I wonder how these verses would have sounded if Abraham and Noah's wives had written the account! I can hear them now, complaining about leaving their comfortable homes for a stinky ark and a wind-blown tent! They probably helped take care of the animals in both situations. Can't you sympathize with their plight? They had to make a home in the worst conditions. I've known modern-day women like them—one who moved with pipeline construction, who kept a piano in a small trailer, and as they moved around the country each child still kept up with music lessons! She also saw to it that the entire family was in church every Sunday. It would have been easy to forget the promises, to lose the faith, to be too busy with the concerns of the world to look for the glory of heaven.

Hebrews tells us that though Abraham lived in tents as a nomad, he was looking for a city with foundations. Only heaven could be this city, whose architect and builder is God! Are you looking for the same city, the golden cube? (We saw this in Study 16.) Read on to see how Abraham received his reward because he had been diligently seeking God, trusting in His promise: "By faith Abraham, even though he was past age—and Sarah herself was barren—was enabled to become a father because he considered him faithful who had made the promise. And so from this one man, and he as good as dead, came descendants as numerous as the stars in the sky and as countless as the sand on the seashore" (Hebrews 11:11–12). What a miracle: an infertile man and woman produced a child, the promise of God!

❧ FRIEND TO FRIEND ❧

Describe a time you were too busy to look forward to heaven or God's promises.

Christian then makes an important point in verse 13: "All these people were still living by faith when they died. They did not receive the things promised; they only saw them and welcomed them from a distance. And they admitted that they were aliens and strangers on earth." As you read these words, are you thinking, "Bummer! How sad! They didn't live to see the promise!"? Never worry. They were gloriously happy when they died . . . because of their faith. "People who say such things [Noah, Abraham, and the others] show that they are looking for a country of their own. If they had been thinking of the country they had left, they would have had opportunity to return. Instead, they were longing for a better country—a heavenly one. Therefore God is not ashamed to be called their God, for he has prepared a city for them" (Hebrews 11:14–16). These faithful patriarchs could have turned back at any time. Noah could have refused to build the ark and died in the flood; Abraham could have lived an uneventful life in Haran, perhaps never having a child—and certainly not reaching the promised land. But they chose to look forward, move out, live by faith.

> "By faith Abraham, when God tested him, offered Isaac as a sacrifice. He who had received the promises was about to sacrifice his one and only son, even though God had said to him, 'It is through Isaac that your offspring will be reckoned.' Abraham reasoned that God could raise the dead, and figuratively speaking, he did receive Isaac back from death. By faith Isaac blessed Jacob and Esau in regard to their future. By faith Jacob, when he was dying, blessed each of Joseph's sons, and worshipped as he leaned on the top of his staff. By faith Joseph, when his end was near, spoke about the exodus of the Israelites from Egypt and gave instructions about his bones"

Not Ability but Availability

Can you imagine how much faith it must have taken for these Old Testament figures to launch out *in faith*? How much faith would you require to move out of your comfort zone and serve God in a new place or by a new pattern? Paul says, "Do not conform any longer to the pattern of this world, but be transformed by the renewing of your mind. . . . For by the grace given me I say to every one of you: . . . think of yourself with sober judgment, *in accordance with the measure of faith God has given you.* Just as each of us has one body with many members, and these members do not all have the same function, so in Christ we who are many form one body, and each member belongs to all the others" (Romans 12:2–5; emphasis mine).

Notice the words in italics above: not *a measure* of faith, assuming that each has a different amount of faith, but *the measure* of faith, assuming (with the definite article *the*) that God has given every person the same measure! If we all have the same measure of faith and we *develop* it to its fullest, we can work together, each in our own way, and accomplish God's will for the world. It doesn't matter whether your faith is weak; what matters is how you use your weak faith for God!

Jesus Himself said that small measures of faith can be astounding: Jesus says, "If you have faith as small as a mustard seed, you can say to this mountain, 'Move from here to there' and it will move. Nothing will be impossible for you" (Matthew 17:20). If you don't have a jar or tin of mustard seeds in your kitchen, buy one today as a reminder of how tiny your faith can be, and still God accepts it as righteousness!

❧ FRIEND TO FRIEND ❧

Continue writing your list (from the beginning of Study 24) of all the persons of faith and what each one did by faith.

Touch My Heart, Lord Jesus

O my faith-giver, I feel so weak before You! May I possess the measure of faith You have given me as evidence and substance of Your love, to trust You daily. As I wander through this life of flux and change, help me seek the city with foundations, where Your presence reigns forever. Today I declare with assurance: I shall go to heaven, in Jesus' name. Amen.

STUDY 25 *Receiving the Promise*
HEBREWS 11:23–40

FROM A COLISEUM SEAT I listened as the president of a denomination told of his encounter with a prostitute on the street. When he began to speak of Jesus, she paid no attention. Then he said, "My wife is just like you."

Wide eyed, the prostitute stared at him, then blinked. "What?"

Sitting in my seat I giggled. I thought of his wife. If she had been nearby, she would have been wide-eyed too!

"Yes," he said. "My wife is a sinner too. And so am I. My wife has been saved by grace. And so have I. And so can you. Would you like to know how?" He began to tell her God's plan of salvation for all—even for prostitutes.

Have you ever considered yourself like a prostitute? How would you compare yourself to one? In today's study God gives a prostitute a high place in the list of persons with faith.

Years have passed since the words in Hebrews 11:22 were written. Sometimes for brevity Scripture commentaries skip over certain verses. Christian, our name for the Hebrews author, condenses history in today's study. Frankly, I'm glad he did, since I get bored reading genealogies. Did you ever feel you were caught in "the begats"? Just try reading Genesis 5, King James Version!

Moses, a Basket Case

After Joseph (Jacob's next to youngest son) died (Hebrews 11:22), the Israelites multiplied and lived in Egypt for generations. Favored living gave way to slavery. Christian picks up the story with the life of one Israelite, Moses. You know the story: how under threat of death to little boys, Moses' mother hid him in a small floating basket hidden by river reeds. "By faith Moses' parents hid him for three months after he was born, because they saw he was no ordinary child, and they were not afraid of the king's edict" (Hebrews 11:23). Christian continues: "By faith Moses, when he had grown up, refused to be known as the son of Pharaoh's daughter. He chose to be mistreated along with the people of God rather than to enjoy the pleasures of sin for a short time. He regarded disgrace for the sake of Christ as of greater value than the treasures of Egypt, because he was looking ahead to his reward" (Hebrews 11:24–26).

Look closely at the last sentence. Moses was mistreated for the sake of *Christ*? Even though Christ had not been born? Does that make sense? Why did Moses allow himself to be mistreated? Christian says Moses was looking ahead. Remember in Study 23 these words? "They were longing for a better country—a heavenly one . . . . God . . . has prepared a city for them" (Hebrews 11:16). Later he says, "we are looking for the city that is to come"

(Hebrews 13:14), our reward in heaven. In a logical world, bound by time and space, Christian's time frame makes no sense here. However, as you look back, you can see the foreshadowing of Christ in every book of the Bible!

Moses looked forward through the eyes of faith, and faith never makes sense in a logical world. Paul says faith is a stumbling block to the Jews and Gentiles (mostly Greeks, the most logical of all groups): "We preach Christ crucified: a stumbling block to Jews and foolishness to Gentiles, but to those whom God has called, both Jews and Greeks, Christ the power of God and the wisdom of God" (1 Corinthians 1:23–24). Faith in Him and His power supersedes all human logic!

✎ FRIEND TO FRIEND ✎

Discuss with a study friend a few things about being a Christian that have been a stumbling block to you.

How did you resolve the doubt the stumbling blocks caused?

How does faith play a part of your everyday life?

Christian continues the story of Moses and the people of faith: "By faith he left Egypt, not fearing the king's anger; he persevered because he saw him who is invisible. By faith he kept the Passover and the sprinkling of blood, so that the destroyer of the firstborn would not touch the firstborn of Israel. By faith the people passed through the Red Sea as on dry land; but when the Egyptians tried to do so, they were drowned. By faith the walls of Jericho fell, after the people had marched around them for seven days. By faith the prostitute Rahab, because she welcomed the spies, was not killed with those who were disobedient" (Hebrews 11:27–31). From the exodus through the settling of the promised land, God provided people of faith, including a prostitute—and He has continued to give us, worthy or not, the measure of faith until this day!

❦ FRIEND TO FRIEND ❦

Read Joshua 2:1–23 and 6:17, 25, selecting Rahab's good qualities.

For extra reading about each person of faith on the list, look up their names in a good Bible concordance. Make notes in the margins of these studies about each one. Share with your study friend things you learn about each of them that apply to your life.

What the List Means to Me

For more of Rahab's story, read Joshua 2:1–23; 6:17, 25. Christian says, "And what more shall I say? I do not have time to tell about Gideon, Barak, Samson, Jephthah, David, Samuel and the prophets, who through faith conquered kingdoms, administered justice, and gained what was promised; who shut the mouths of lions, quenched the fury of the flames, and escaped the edge of the sword; whose weakness was turned to strength; and who became powerful in battle and routed foreign armies. Women received back their dead, raised to life again. Others were tortured and refused to be released, so that they might gain a better resurrection. Some faced jeers and flogging, while still others were chained and put in prison. They were stoned; they were sawed in two; they were put to death by the sword. They went about in sheepskins and goatskins, destitute, persecuted and mistreated—the world was not worthy of them. They wandered in deserts and mountains, and in caves and holes in the ground. These were all commended for their faith, yet none of them received what had been promised" (Hebrews 11:32–39). This passage is so powerful that it brings me to tears. I remember my pastor, Dr. Russell Dean, preaching on this passage of Scripture when I lived in Clinton, South Carolina. He said that if you do not believe in the resurrection of Jesus, one thing should convince you: the people of faith who have been willing to die for it.

Faith is something that doesn't meet the eye at first; it is deeper than life. Once you notice people of faith, you see something different about them, something *better* about them, something that makes them say, "*Forsaking All, I Trust Him.*" Can you say that? Or do you worry about where your next meal is coming from, how your children will do in school today, what will happen to your bank account, your house, your car, your family, your jewelry, your appliances, your church . . . ? The list goes on. You can make a list of faith or a list of worry. The choice is up to you.

Would you like to add people to this list of faith? List here persons you believe God has listed, folks written in the Book of Life in heaven, because you saw faith in them. Share with your study friend why you included these persons.

Looking for Something Better

Just as these individual persons of faith were looking forward, not backward, you can also look toward heaven every day. A long time ago God planned something better for you, too. "God had planned something better for us so that only together with us would they be made perfect" (Hebrews 11:40). As we've already seen, study after study, Jesus is the "something better." When He died as a once-for-all/ One-for-all sacrifice, He died for everyone on the list you've compiled. At the moment of His resurrection the promise was sure. We don't know absolutely, but it's possible Christian saw in person the miracle of Jesus, and he claimed that hope and promise, looking forward to the future with his Lord! You have that same promise today, if you are a person of faith. The Old Testament patriarchs, the New Testament apostles, along with other persons of faith through the years, will join you in heaven as all of us are made perfect in Christ!

Touch My Heart, Lord Jesus
O faithful God, thank You for these examples of faith! Forgive me when I condemn people like Rahab; may I always see good in others. I am also thankful for those in my life who lived as examples for me. Like them, may I be found faithful, Lord. May I live a life of hope every day—not bound by time and space, but looking forward to heaven. Amen.

UNIT 6 *I'm Better, Not Bitter*

AT LAST, GODLY WOMAN, you are approaching the final studies in this book. You're almost finished "running the race marked out for us," as Christian says. In the last few chapters of Hebrews, you will learn how to keep your eyes on Jesus, avoid getting weary, and accept the discipline you need. Again, as in other places in Hebrews, you'll be able to celebrate your holiness without embarrassment. You'll explore ways to live in peace and avoid bitterness. Receiving an unshakable kingdom, you can worship God acceptably. There are even two places where these studies give you marital advice and help you with financial worries!

We'll get real in this unit. We'll talk about suffering outside your comfort zone to identify with Jesus. Finally, we'll explore how you can continually offer the sacrifice of praise and stand in awe of our God, who takes your breath away! Does that sound like something you'd like to do? Then go for it! Turn the page and begin!

STUDY 26 *Better Discipline, a Way of Love*
HEBREWS 12:1–13

Hebrews 12
Since we're surrounded by great clouds
Of witnesses t'our earthly plight,
Then let us throw off hind'ring shrouds
And sin that haunts us in the night.

And let us run and persevere
The race that is before us now.
And keep our eyes on Jesus near
The author, finisher! See His brow!

The brow of Him, God's only Son,
Who bore the marks of bloody thorn,
Who for the joy God let Him run,
Endured the cross, its shame to scorn.

And closer up toward God we grow,
Who disciplines us day by day.
He guides us as we love Him so
And from Mount Zion shows the way.

—EDNA M. ELLISON, © 2002

Here's another chapter that begins with therefore: "Therefore, since we are surrounded by such a great cloud of witnesses, let us throw off everything that hinders and the sin that so easily entangles, and let us run with perseverance the race marked out for us" (Hebrews 12:1). I breathe a great sigh of relief as I read this therefore. At last we've come to the end of the list of faith! Here's the way Eugene Peterson paraphrases this verse: "Do you see what this means—all these pioneers who blazed the way, all these veterans cheering us on? It means we'd better get on with it! Strip down, start running—and never quit! No extra spiritual fat, no parasitic sins" (Hebrews 12:1 *The Message*).

We're running a race for others to see. Paul says we are in a giant arena, where Christians are on display: "We have been made a spectacle to the whole universe, to angels as well as to men" (1 Corinthians 4:9). When he considers the cloud of witnesses, Billy Graham asks, "How would you live if you knew that you were being watched all the time?" He cites 1 Corinthians 4:9 in the Amplified Bible: "God has made an exhibit of us . . . [a show in the world's amphitheater] with both men and angels [as spectators]."

He says, "We know they are watching, but in the heat of the battle, I have thought how wonderful it would be if we could hear them cheering." Don't you wish you could see and hear Moses and Noah, with a few angels beside them—along with your great Uncle Charles—sitting in the stands watching your life, encouraging you to do your best? What a sight!

What two things should you do, since others are cheering you on in this race?

1.

2.

What are your hindrances?

Write here your possible plans for getting rid of them:

Which sins entangle you?

⚜ FRIEND TO FRIEND ⚜

Which of the following are the easiest for you:

throw off hindrances

run a race

persevere

Share your possibilities and plans with your study friend.

Don't Lose Heart

Christian suggests you do two things, as others cheer you on: (1) throw off things that hinder you, and (2) run with perseverance. Easy for him to say! Throwing away all my sins and running the Christian 500 without getting out of breath—ministering to others without growing weary—is hard to do! I'd say it's impossible except for the next verses; here's the only way I know to do it: "Let us fix our eyes on Jesus, the author and perfecter of our faith, who for the joy set before him endured the Cross, scorning its shame, and sat down at the right hand of the throne of God. Consider him who endured such opposition from sinful men, so that you will not grow weary and lose heart. In your struggle against sin, you have not yet resisted to the point of shedding your blood. And you have forgotten that word of encouragement that addresses you as sons: 'My son, do not make light of the Lord's discipline, and do not lose heart when he rebukes you, because the Lord disciplines those he loves, and he punishes everyone he accepts as a son.' Endure hardship as discipline; God is treating you as sons. For what son is not disciplined by his father?" (Hebrews 12:2–7).

Christian's advice is (1) keep your eyes on Jesus, (2) don't get weary, and (3) accept discipline. One period of my life stands out in my memory as a time I did all three of those. My son, Jack, had been in an automobile accident, breaking his hip in three parts. It took an 11-hour operation, 35 plates, and 36 pins to put him back together. The hardest part of recovery for me took place after he left the main hospital and then the rehabilitation hospital, but still returned for physical therapy. After work I helped him to the car, folded the heavy wheelchair, placed it in the trunk, drove him to the rehab clinic, lifted the wheelchair out of the trunk, unfolded it, and helped him wheel the endless corridors to the therapy area. Later, we'd repeat the process, finally lifting the wheelchair out of the trunk one last time and helping Jack into the house for the night.

An amazing thing happened. For years I had suffered lower back pain, especially after a long plane or car ride. During the days of Jack's recuperation, all the pain disappeared. I finally figured it out. My back pain was probably caused by the lack of exercise in my sedentary office job. The exercise that I thought was torture—all the lifting—was strengthening my back, healing my body. I've never had back trouble since!

No Pain, No Gain

I've always said I don't believe in the motto, "No pain, no gain." (A sadist must have written it!) However, I have seen the principle in action several times in my life, and it worked! Christian believed in that principle, too. He gives us reasons for discipline in the next verses: "If you are not disciplined (and everyone undergoes discipline), then you are illegitimate children and not true sons. Moreover, we have all had human fathers who disciplined us and we respected them for it. How much more should we submit to the Father of our spirits and live! Our fathers disciplined us for a little while as they thought best; but God disciplines us for our good, that we may share in his holiness" (Hebrews 12:8–10). I must admit Jack was a true son. From ages three to five, he had timeout so many times that "Jack's corner" was kept busy—and that was before the days of timeout! Christian reminds us of the Scriptures in Deuteronomy 8:5. We have been called sons, or daughters, of God, who tends to us, lovingly nudging us in the right direction for our own good. We are not to laugh at God or to lose heart when times are tough. Part of our faith is trusting that He is doing everything in our lives for our own good.

❧ FRIEND TO FRIEND ❧

Are you in a time of discipline now? Discuss with your study friend.

What have your learned during hard times in your life?

What are you learning now?

Here's the Gain: Share in His Holiness!

Christian says, "No discipline seems pleasant at the time, but painful. Later on, however, it produces a harvest of righteousness and peace for those who have been trained by it" (Hebrews 12:11). Have you seen a harvest of righteousness because of some discipline God has led you through? Are you now in a period of discipline, eager for the harvest? If so, God can encourage you with these words: "Therefore, strengthen your feeble arms and weak knees. 'Make level paths for your feet,' so that the lame may not be disabled, but rather healed" (Hebrews 12:12–13). God wants you to walk on a path toward Him, not toward destruction. He says, "Make level paths for your feet and take only ways that are firm" (Proverbs 4:26). We close our study today with these comforting instructions from our Lord. In the next study we will learn to watch out for others on the path.

Touch My Heart, Lord Jesus

Father, thank You for disciplining me as Your child. I know You nudge me in the right direction as a loving parent disciplines a child, because You take delight in me and want me to run on a firm path. May I throw off things that hinder me and keep going, as others cheer me on! Amen.

STUDY 27 *Bitter Roots, Without the Terror*
HEBREWS 12:14–29

ON THE LAST NIGHT of girls' camp in North Carolina, comfortable in a staff cabin, I heard a thunderstorm coming. I looked out the window: staff cabins on our hill, quiet . . . at the bottom of the hill, cabins holding 300 little girls, all quiet. Susan, the other staff member in the room, was sleeping. I decided to pray. How happy I was that the storm was moving away, diminishing with each rumble.

"Well," I heard Susan say in the dark, "the thunderstorm is leaving."

"Yes," I laughed. "I thought you were asleep. I was doing some fervent praying! I thought I might need to go check on the girls, and you know what my bathrobe looks like! I don't want anyone to see this mangy thing."

She laughed. "It looks like . . ."

"It looks like a mangy dog. The chenille used to be pink and fluffy, but it's now gray and frazzled. Add my matted, dirty-gray fuzzy bedroom slippers—which used to be pink—the girls will die laughing! With the first thunder, I prayed, 'God, don't send me down the hill to calm the girls, with my umbrella like a lightning rod on this high hill! I'm scared of tornado-storms like that one, but more than that, I'm scared of campers seeing me in this ragged bathrobe and slippers!' I know God answered my prayer and turned the storm."

After a pause, Susan said, "You Christian types make me sick. You know that?"

I was stunned. I had assumed Susan was a Christian, since she was on staff at a Christian camp.

"You think you can just snap your fingers and God answers you. What if a farmer on the other side of the mountain prayed for rain?"

I started to answer, and then Susan fired hard questions at me, like, "How do you explain the virgin birth, anyway?" and "If a pygmy in the jungle never heard of Jesus, and he's a good man, is he going to hell when he dies?"

I tried to answer, but felt inadequate. I stammered, telling her what I had learned in my church—that we were responsible for everyone hearing about Jesus—but she was not satisfied. Finally I said, "Susan, I have found that people who pick over some small doctrine or question the truth in the Bible are really avoiding the real question: their own sin."

Dead silence in that dark room.

Then Susan said, "Yes, I have sinned, but probably not more than you have."

"You're right," I said. "All of us have sinned." Suddenly I realized I was standing right on Romans 3:23, "All have sinned and fall short of the glory of God," a beginning verse to the plan of salvation, which a Christian might use to lead someone to Jesus as Savior. I breathed heavily.

"Not my mother," she said. "My mother was a good person. She loved me unselfishly all my life . . . and she died this year . . .and she was not a Christian . . . and, Edna, you're not going to tell me my mother is burning in hell tonight!" Susan began to cry.

We heard a knock at the door, and I ran out. Whew! I was glad a little girl frightened by the storm needed me to tuck her in. I left as fast as I could—without my umbrella, but wrapping my mangy robe around me, glad to get away from Susan.

After settling the child in her bunk, I returned, stopping in the bath-house on the way. As I washed my hands in the long tin sink, I said, "God, if You could arrange it, would You let Susan be asleep when I go in? I've not done a good job of witnessing; I made her cry, and I'm sure her pastor or someone could do a better job for You than I've done. Unless You nudge her in the dark before I go in, I won't say a word."

Good. The room was quiet when I entered. Susan was asleep. I tip-toed across the room and put one knee up to hop into the bunk.

"Edna?" It was Susan.

I froze in position, with one leg hiked up on the bed. "Yes?"

"God nudged me in the dark. He spoke to me while you were gone."
Silence.

"Well, don't you want to know what He said?" she asked.

"Yes." My heart was pounding. I stood on that foot, paralyzed.

"God said, 'Susan, don't worry about your mother. I'll take care of that. You need to think of your own heart . . . what you will do with Jesus.'"

I lowered my foot and walked over to Susan's bunk. I knew she was ready.

She was broken before God, ready to receive Jesus as her Savior. I knelt down beside her bed and explained the plan of salvation: "God is a just God who punishes sin and rewards goodness. We'd want Him to be just, wouldn't we, to keep law and order? He always brings justice."

She nodded.

"Yet God also loves you, Susan, more than anything. He wants a relationship with all of us, because He loves us. Since our sins (and there are many of them; all of us have committed them) keep us apart from a holy God, He had a dilemma: on one hand He had to punish sin. On the other hand, He loved us and did not want us to suffer. The answer to that dilemma is Jesus. He came from heaven to earth as God incarnate, to suffer death on the Cross as our sacrificial Lamb. He died in our place, for our sins. He offers that forgiveness and redemption right now. Would you like to say yes, trusting Jesus alone for your salvation from punishment and for your entrance into heaven when you die?"

Susan answered, "Yes, I would." She knew God loved her and then repeated after me a prayer of assurance. What a miracle happened that night! Susan left camp the next morning for a weeklong health spa. She wrote to me: "Dear Edna, thank you for showing me how much Jesus loves me. I have been so happy all week. I am in a building with 12 Jewish women, and I've just about Christianized every one of them!"

What a happy ending to the story! Not only had Susan met her Savior face to face, but also her joy in salvation had flowed out into the lives of 12 other women! She began a life without worry, resting in the arms of Jesus.

Live the New Life

Christian knew what Susan learned that night. She was afraid of being holy. Because her mother had not known Jesus as Savior, her loyalty to her mother prevented her being the godly woman God wanted her to be. Christian says, "Make every effort to live in peace with all men and to be holy; without holiness no one will see the Lord" (Hebrews 12:14).

As if you could do that!

Christian asks only the impossible: (1) live in peace and (2) be holy. Riiiiiight. These are two things I've tried to do all my life, and—I tell you—on this earth, it's simply impossible! How easy will it be for you to do these two things? I'm sitting in my bedroom, dressed in sweats with a hole in the shoulder, with the computer screen bright in my face, afraid to look in the mirror for the frightening view of my hairdo and outfit! To tell the truth, I don't feel so holy today. I couldn't even find my halo in this messy office area! How about you?

As if these weren't enough, here's another suggestion: "See to it that no one misses the grace of God and that no bitter root grows up to cause trouble and defile many" (Hebrews 12:15). Besides the two commands above, here are two more:

Don't let anyone miss the grace.

Don't allow bitterness.

❧ FRIEND TO FRIEND ❧

How well do you follow these commands? Discuss with your study partner.

These are huge commands. *Huge!* You are responsible for others missing the grace. As you live in peace, you become holy through Christ. It's impossible for you to live in peace and be holy on your own. You do those only through Him. Then you can tend to others and care for them, as He cares for you, without any bitterness or jealousy. We should wear t-shirts that say: "No Bitterness Allowed." Should that sign be put up above the doors of your church, and mine as well? The next verse follows the same pattern: "See that no one is sexually immoral, or is godless like Esau, who for a single meal sold his inheritance rights as the oldest son" (Hebrews 12:16). Here are two more commands:

Don't be immoral. (Beware of sexual immorality!) and

Don't be godless. (If that means casual, or irreverent, then God is stepping on my toes at the moment!)

He explains what happened to Esau (Isaac's son, in Genesis 25:29–34 and 27:30–40, who sold his birthright to his twin, Jacob): "Afterward, as you know, when he wanted to inherit this blessing, he was rejected. He could bring about no change of mind, though he sought the blessing with tears" (Hebrews 12:17). God gives us opportunities to be moral—and serious about serving Him—and after a certain point, we can't retract the moment of opportunity that is lost. We can get stuck in the mire of everyday life and be bogged down in unholiness, disgrace, bitterness, immorality, and godlessness. Shakespeare said,

> There is a tide in the affairs of men
> Which, taken at the flood, leads on to fortune;
> Omitted, all the voyage of their life
> Is bound in shallows and in miseries.
> —*Julius Caesar*, IV, iii

Don't be stuck in the mud! As God gives you opportunity, do good. Serve Him with all your heart and soul and mind and strength!

Flee the Old Terror

Christian contrasts his day with a time when Moses faced God at Mount Sinai, in the days of the Old Covenant/Old Testament: "You have not come to a mountain that can be touched and that is burning with fire; to darkness, gloom and storm; to a trumpet blast or to such a voice speaking words that those who heard it begged that no further word be spoken to them, because they could not bear what was commanded: 'If even an animal touches the mountain, it must be stoned.' The sight was so terrifying that Moses said, 'I am trembling with fear'" (Hebrews 12:18–21). The words, sight, and presence of God are awesome! He was fierce as He related to the Israelites during the exodus, but you may live under a new relationship with Him. You don't ever need to be frightened by God. He will not take advantage of you or violate your trust. Read on!

Come to Mt. Zion

On the other hand, Hebrews 12:22 points us to heaven: "But you have come to Mount Zion, to the heavenly Jerusalem, the city of the living God. You have come to thousands upon thousands of angels in joyful assembly, to the church of the firstborn, whose names are written in heaven. You have come to God, the judge of all men, to the spirits of righteous men made perfect, to Jesus the mediator of a new covenant, and to the sprinkled blood that speaks a better word than the blood of Abel" (Hebrews 12:22–24). Abel, the son of Adam and Eve, was killed by his brother, Cain, the first murderer. Christian's words are poetic here: Jesus' blood speaks a better word than Abel's blood. Jesus, the Better Way, leads us to peace in heaven; Abel led us to warfare on earth, brother against brother.

What does Jesus' blood say about you?

Don't Refuse Him. Listen . . .

"See to it that you do not refuse him who speaks. If they did not escape when they refused him who warned them on earth, how much less will we, if we turn away from him who warns us from heaven?" (Hebrews 12:25) How do you listen to God? You must hear beyond the spoken word. Your two ears are not enough to enable you to really listen—to God or anyone else. Turn your eyes toward Jesus in warm eye contact. Wait for the soft touch. Reach out and touch His Holy Spirit. Experience gentle silence, nod your head, and agree in your heart. Practice real listening, as you read His Word and pray daily.

Review the commands of God in Hebrews 12. Which are easier? Which are harder? Share your feelings about following each of the commands with your study friend:

1. Live in peace.
2. Be holy.
3. Don't let anyone miss the grace.
4. Don't allow bitterness.
5. Don't be immoral.
6. Don't be godless.
7. Flee your old terrors.
8. Listen to God.
9. Don't worry.
10. Be thankful.
11. Worship with awe.

Share your answers with your study partner.

Trust the Unshakable Kingdom

"At that time his voice shook the earth, but now he has promised, 'Once more I will shake not only the earth but also the heavens.' The words 'once more' indicate the removing of what can be shaken—that is, created things—so that what cannot be shaken may remain" (Hebrews 12:26–27). If all else falls around you, Jesus will still be strong. Permanent. Loving. Merciful. Our God is unshakable.

Don't Worry; Be Thankful

Someone told me recently, "Worry is the interest paid on trouble before it is due," but during the Cuban missile crisis, when my son, Jack, was two, I worried! I was several hours away from home on a shopping trip when I realized the United States might be entering World War III. I knew I showed distrust for God when I worried, but in a time of panic, I didn't consider what I knew, only what I felt. I hurried back to my child, hugged my family, and stayed close for the next few weeks. After that crisis was over, I felt I could endure anything. Looking back, I realized that surviving the winter of 1961–62, two years before the missile crisis—at home with a baby, cleaning and washing a ton of cloth baby diapers—was the real crisis for me. Scrubbing, bleaching, bluing, hanging clothes outside in windy, below-freezing weather, only to begin again the next day . . . a little one with fever, jaundice, rashes . . . those were rough days. God taught me great volumes from His Spirit in those tender years that have steadied me for many future years with Him. No matter what, I will not worry. God's kingdom cannot be shaken.

Worship with Awe

Christian ends on a cheerful note: "Therefore, since we are receiving a kingdom that cannot be shaken, let us be thankful, and so worship God acceptably with reverence and awe, for our 'God is a consuming fire'" (Hebrews 12:28–29). Because the kingdom of heaven, which lives in your heart, cannot be shaken, give thanks.

Touch My Heart, Lord Jesus

Awesome God, help me to be holy through the Holy Spirit's refining of my heart. Help me live in peace without bitterness. Don't let loyalty to others, conformity, lust, or terror lead me into immorality, godlessness, or worry. Help me to listen to You, merciful Lord. You are all that stands when all else fails. With a thankful heart, I worship You with awe. Amen.

STUDY 28 *Better Love, a Promise to Keep*
HEBREWS 13:1–8

Hebrews 13
Oh, brother, sister in the race,
Reach out to angels unaware;
For hearts are strengthened by His grace;
Now band together; show you care.

Let's imitate our leaders old;
Let's bear disgrace that Jesus bore;
Let's look for heaven, be so bold
That we can find strength—even more!

Now offer Him the sacrifice
Of praise and love forever more!
Find work a joy! Be kind, be nice,
Be prayerful. Think of what's in store!

And may the God of peace and love
Equip you each so you won't fall,
And grant you honor from above
And grace unending with you all.

—EDNA M. ELLISON, © 2002

Paul Hood was a co-worker of mine for seven years. When my nephew Brant had to have a kidney mass removed, I was concerned and asked people in our work place to pray for him. As soon as he heard, Paul came to me to assure me Brant would be healthy with only one kidney. Paul himself had only one. I asked what had happened to his other kidney. To my surprise, he told me he had given it to his sister! Years before, his sister needed a kidney transplant, and Paul had quickly donated his. He told me that no amount of pain or surgical procedure was too bad to endure in exchange for his dear sister. He would have given her one lung and one eye, as well!

Your Love and His
Today's study brings us to the last chapter of Hebrews, one that concentrates on Christian love: "Keep on loving each other as brothers. Do not forget to entertain strangers, for by so doing some people have entertained angels without knowing it" (Hebrews 13:1–2). This verse has two important commands: (1) love each other and (2) entertain strangers. Look at

verse 1. How do brothers (or sisters) love? Christian acknowledges that the Hebrews are already loving each other; he just asks them to keep it up! If you have a brother or a sister, how do you love them?

I have one sister, Phyllis, who is a joy to be around. In our family, we ask, "Is Phyllis going to the party?" If she is, we decide to go, because we know it will always be fun! She knows how to laugh with abandon! She was born when I was ten, and I welcomed her home from the hospital as a new doll to play with and take care of. Nothing was more fun than watching her learn to eat, play hopscotch, or ride a bike. I watched with horror one day as she rode her tricycle off the porch, cutting her eyebrow area as she hit some rocks ten feet below. As the doctor stitched her up, I realized how precious she was to me. She will always be younger than I, but we joke about who is the older. She will always weigh less than I (she's several inches shorter, with a smaller bone structure), but we joke about who is the heaviest. She has beautiful curly black hair, which will always be darker than mine, because I have a ten-year head start on the gray hairs peeking through! We know a few inside jokes that no one else understands. We shared a mother, father, and brother who have died. Nothing could separate us from our bond except death itself.

Phyllis's most admired quality is her Christian service. She acts out her faith by playing the organ at her church—every Sunday morning, Sunday night, and Wednesday night. She is a faithful pray-er for sick and troubled people. She takes children to church with her and encourages youth. She's been on many mission trips and is faithful to share those experiences with others. She's my sister in Christ as well as my physical sister, and that deepens our bond!

Is Phyllis perfect? No more than I am, but I don't see any of her flaws. I see only my little sister, whom I love with all my heart. Mother used to say, "Blood is thicker than water," and that saying is true with Phyllis—and with Christ.

❧ FRIEND TO FRIEND ❧

Describe your siblings as I described Phyllis. What makes you close to them?

How do you wish you were closer?

With your study friend, discuss ways to become closer.

Entertain Strangers

Look at Hebrews 13:2. Why does Christian say you should entertain strangers? From time to time, have you encountered folks who just seemed to stay for a few moments or days and then faded out of your life? Have you ever entertained angels without
knowing it?

Christian continues: "Remember those in prison as if you were their fellow prisoners, and those who are mistreated as if you yourselves were suffering" (Hebrews 1:3). [There's that prison topic again!]. Today you and I should be concerned not only for the Christians who suffer persecution for their faith, but also for all prisoners, their families, and prison staff. Our system of justice, based on God-given principles, is one of the best in the world, but it has much that needs changing. You can be an advocate for youth offenders, for children of mothers in prison, and for those serving time in jail.

❧ FRIEND TO FRIEND ❧

Under each category, write two simple actions you can take to minister to prisoners, their families, or their institutions' staff:

Visits:

Ministries:

Prayer:

Share your plans with your study friend.

Christian then warns the Hebrews: "Marriage should be honored by all, and the marriage bed kept pure, for God will judge the adulterer and all the sexually immoral" (Hebrews 13:4). Can it be any plainer than that? God will judge your sexual immorality. If you have any impure thought, nip it in the bud before it becomes action. Today Christian might say, "Guard your heart. Guard your computer. Guard your magazines. Guard your television. Guard your friendships. Don't let any sexual filth into your home, school, or work place! Watch out for friendships that you know may lead to sexual tension or arousal. Satan looks for God's choicest Christians, and then attacks."

Christian adds another warning: "Keep your lzives free from the love of money and be content with what you have, because God has said, 'Never will I leave you; never will I forsake you'" (Hebrews 13:5).

✣ FRIEND TO FRIEND ✣

In Hebrews 13:5, what two actions does Christian ask you to take?

What promise(s) did God pledge to you?

A pastor who had never made more than $8,000 per year asked a financial counselor, "Can I retire?" The financial expert answered, "You can do anything you want to do. Will you adopt me?" The secret to the pastor's giant retirement fund was that he had always spent less than he earned. Although he had made a small salary, he had lived within his means and, over the long haul, had accumulated enough to retire in comfort. Can you be content with what you have? If so, you can live the good life! In this verse, what does "forsake" mean? Jesus says, "I will never renounce you, toss you aside like an old habit I don't plan to resume." You can be confident that God will take care of you. Because (1) you can be content with God, then (2) you can be confident with life. "So we say with confidence, 'The Lord is my helper; I will not be afraid. What can man do to me?'" (Hebrews 13:6).

Yesterday, Today, and Forever

Christian says, "Remember your leaders, who spoke the word of God to you. Consider the outcome of their way of life and imitate their faith. Jesus Christ is the same yesterday and today and forever" (Hebrews 13:7–8). Whose life or faith should you imitate? Through the years, people have gone before you who trusted Jesus as their Savior and guide. Those who cheer you on knew the truth. You can learn from them. Set aside today as a day of remembrance. Spend a few moments now thanking God for people who lived before you, whose example you can follow. May you live an even more exemplary life than they did, as you follow in their footsteps! The same Jesus whom they followed faithfully is the One, the Only One you follow to live out the same principles of faith! Hallelujah! Time does not matter! He's the same yesterday, today, and forever!

Share with your study friend your good memories of Christians who influenced your faith.

Write on the time line below the names of Christians who have influenced you, are influencing you, or are likely to influence you in the future.

TIME LINE

Past	Now	Future

Touch My Heart, Lord Jesus

Lord Jesus, thank You for the influence of faithful Christians on my life. Help me to continue to love others like my sisters and brothers. May I always live within my means so I can be able to show hospitality to strangers and prisoners. Keep my marriage—or the marriages of those around me—pure. I am confident in You, O Lord of yesterday, today, and forever! Amen.

STUDY 29 *Better Living, Outside the Camp*
HEBREWS 13:9–19

AS WE APPROACH this next-to-the-last study, Christian, our name for the writer of Hebrews, continues to encourage us. He gives us practical advice for staying on the Christian path as we live on earth, looking for heaven. Sometimes even strong Christians can stray, listening to the wrong voices and taking the wrong fork in the road.

Sometimes we take the wrong path just because the world we live in makes no sense. I just stopped my computer by clicking on the Start button. Why don't computer screens have a Stop button? We must hit the Start button to turn the machine off. We go through life doing a series of goofy things: we drive on the parkway and park on the driveway; we can be "climbing the walls," even if we're not near any real walls; and we can be "tickled to death" to do something, even when no one tickles us or we don't come anywhere near death!

In the midst of this confusion, our awesome God stands firm. Sometimes you praise Him as you pray, read your Bible, or study a book like this. Sometimes you meet the awesome God when you find ministry to do. Sometimes other Christians along the way encourage you. Sometimes, if you're like me, you don't have a clue what God is doing, even when He is working miracles all around you!

When I lived in Birmingham, Betty Morgan and her husband, Charles, were good friends to me and my son when we were new in town. Betty, Faye Knight, Stella Bryant, and others are missions-hearted women who keep looking for the wonder. They don't just sit at home and dream about it; they move out to the unlikely places and find an awesome Savior there, who takes their breath away! Most of the time I was amazed at what God did through them.

One day Betty called to ask if I'd like to be trained to teach English as a second language. Duh! I hadn't thought of it, but the training sounded good, especially after she reminded me of how many new Chinese, Mexican, and Japanese restaurants had been built in our community—and none of the workers seemed to speak English. (If we asked for a drink of water, servers scurried to the front desk, returning with a manager fluent in English.) I had to admit my "Duh" syndrome, and I followed Betty out of town for special training. Later we asked someone to come to our church to teach us everything we needed to know. Soon we had 35 students from many countries meeting in our church every Wednesday night. I loved my students and showed up eagerly on Wednesday nights. I had no dream beyond that. Duh!

Betty, on the other hand, looked outside the church again for opportunities. One day she heard that one of the children in our English classes, Alonzo Garcia, had accepted Christ as his Savior during Vacation Bible School.

She said, "Shouldn't we visit his parents?"

As usual, I responded: "Duh, uh, yes, I guess we should. Why?"

"To tell his parents what this means and see if they want to know Jesus too!"

"Oh, yeah . . . duh . . . uh . . . of course!"

Betty, two other friends (Kathy Browne and Sue Carver), and I had learned to witness in a six-week course at church. As we learned how to tell people about Jesus and heaven, we had stepped out in faith, visiting people in the neighborhood. I knew how to witness; I just hadn't thought of doing much of it. "Duh."

Betty already had planned the evening with Alonzo's parents. She said, "I'll take care of their new baby while you witness."

"What?"

"You witness."

"OK."

Why did I say that? I thought. *Babies always love me. I could have done that job and Betty could have witnessed. Besides, I'm fatter than she is; my lap and shoulders are softer for a baby. Duh. Why didn't I tell her that?*

As we had learned to do, we paused outside the Garcias' apartment and prayed that the Holy Spirit would go before us. I prayed for the baby to love Betty. She prayed for my words. My *words* . . . duh . . . I began to think of what I would say. I need not have been concerned. As soon as I began to share about Jesus, Alonzo came over to his father. "Papa! I know what this lady's talking about. It's easy. If God speaks to you, you just say, 'Yes!'"

His father, who had listened intently, was ready to say yes—and much to my surprise, so was Alonzo's mother! Just at the moment I asked, "And would you like to ask Jesus into your heart right now?" the baby, who had been asleep, woke up crying. Betty knew what to do. She calmly picked up the baby, held him close, and he went back to sleep. I asked the question again, and both Alonzo's parents accepted Jesus into their hearts! I sat there in amazement as they prayed. Duh.

I have rarely been so happy! We laughed. We cried. We hugged each other. We promised to keep in touch. As we started to leave, Betty lifted the baby and tried to hand him to his mother. He clung to her and did not want to go back to his mother's arms!

Back in the car, I said, "Betty! I can't handle the joy! Wow! Two people born into the kingdom of God tonight, and He allowed us to be there! Did you see how that baby loved you? He wouldn't even go to his own mother! Yea, God!"

"Edna," she said calmly, "we prayed. God did what we asked Him to do!"

Don't Be Fooled

What happened that night was the heart of the gospel. Sometimes you may be confused by distractions that keep you from doing what God would have you do. You may listen to people who teach you about complicated doctrines, elaborate rituals of worship, or confusing rules of diet, which they say are necessary to be a Christian. However, Christian says, "Do not be carried away by all kinds of strange teachings. It is good for our hearts to be strengthened by grace, not by ceremonial foods, which are of no value to those who eat them" (Hebrew 13:9). As we said in the introduction to this book, Hebrews was written directly to the "Jesus-and" Christians, for those who have the mistaken ideas that we must believe in Jesus-and-angels, Jesus-and-Moses, or Jesus-and-priesthood. Though the Jews (and some Christians) in the first century and even today observe dietary rules and observe special rituals, those things are not the thing. The most important thing is the grace of Jesus, Lord of your life!

A few months after Alonzo's parents became Christians, they asked me about a new Christian group that had been cultivating their friendship. This group had told them they needed to complete a long list of dietary and cultural rules before they could go to heaven. I was glad I could tell them their life in heaven was assured. All we need is Jesus!

Paul says, "The kingdom of God is not a matter of eating and drinking, but of righteousness, peace and joy in the Holy Spirit" (Romans 14:17). For extra reading on New Testament dietary thought, you may want to study 1 Corinthians 8:1 to 10:33. Paul summarizes: "So whether you eat or drink or whatever you do, do it all for the glory of God" (1 Corinthians 10:31).

❧ FRIEND TO FRIEND ❧

What are strange teachings? Which kinds of sects or cults should you avoid?

What are your add-ons to the gospel? Do you believe in Jesus alone for salvation, or do you believe that Jesus-and-education, Jesus-and-cleanliness, Jesus-and-"being good" will get you to heaven? Why or why not?

With what are you strengthened, according to Hebrews 13:9?

Discuss with your study friend your answers to the questions on this page.

God commands us to beware of false priests or false christs. You can be sure that anyone who claims to be Christ, or the Son of God, is not legitimate. Only those who have a living relationship with Jesus and humbly stand before their Lord have a right to eat at His table. Christian says, "We have an altar from which those who minister at the tabernacle have no right to eat" (Hebrews 13:10).

Go Outside the Camp

Next Christian tells another difference between the false priests and Jesus: "The high priest carries the blood of animals into the Most Holy Place as a sin offering, but the bodies are burned outside the camp. And so Jesus also suffered outside the city gate to make the people holy through his own blood. Let us, then, go to him outside the camp, bearing the disgrace he bore" (Hebrews 13:11—13). Jesus was crucified in a horrible place, at Calvary, on a hill called Golgotha, outside the walls of Jerusalem. It was not a popular place where Jews could find all the social graces. The proud priests certainly did not hang out there! However, there they could find Grace personified outside the gates of formal religious laws, as Jesus became the sacrifice for all of us. As the ultimate sacrifice, He identified with the sacrifice itself, not with the luxury.

If you want to identify with Jesus, you will move out of the middle of religious rites—outside the gates, or the doors of the church—and into the places where real people live. You will want to move among the poor, the beggars, the homeless, the sick, and the disabled. As you deepen your relationship with Him, you will gain courage to turn against social acceptance and dare to stand for Him. If you bear disgrace because you are determined to serve your Savior at all costs, then where do you turn? You look for the eternal, not for the moment-by-moment gratification. Christian says, "For here we do not have an enduring city, but we are looking for the city that is to come" (Hebrews 13:14).

Hallelujah! I'm glad I'm looking forward. Aren't you?

Many times I've said to my children when they were concerned about hurt feelings or other pain: "This, too, shall pass. The only thing that's sure, without disgrace, is heaven." Now when either their friends or family have a problem, I hear them telling others: "This, too, shall pass. The only thing that is sure, without disgrace, is heaven." They usually add: "You can make it. I'll stand by you. Hang on!" Watch what you say; it comes back to you in the next generation.

❧ FRIEND TO FRIEND ❧

In your own words, define these two words:
Grace

Disgrace

What kind of disgrace have Christians experienced through the centuries?

How do you (or could you) bear Jesus' disgrace?

How have you observed the "looking forward" theme in Hebrews?

How have you shared with others this principle?

What have you discovered, when you endured hardships by depending on eternal, not temporary things?

What are you looking forward to, in the near or distant future?

Sacrifice of Praise

One way you walk outside the camp is to praise God. Have you noticed that not too many people are pleased when you seem happy all the time? They may think you are a "goody two-shoes," a "Pollyanna," or a foolish person—unrealistic, without any backbone. Remaining optimistic in spite of pain or scorn is not the norm. However, Christian tells us how to live outside the worldly norm: "Through Jesus, therefore, let us continually offer to God a sacrifice of praise—the fruit of lips that confess his name" (Hebrews 13:15).

One of my favorite people constantly says, "Praise the Lord!" When I first heard her say it, I was embarrassed. Then I realized I had fallen into the trap of the world. I have set as a character goal to be bold in saying "Praise the Lord" when appropriate. I am ashamed to say that a few folks still intimidate me so I can't say it in their presence. I'm working on that flaw in my Christian character.

✒ FRIEND TO FRIEND ✒

Share what you've learned about enduring disgrace or hardships with your study friend.

According to Hebrews 13:15, when should you offer a sacrifice of praise?

To whom do you offer it?

Through whom do you offer it?

What kind of fruit do you offer as a sacrifice? From where does this sacrifice come?

It Takes Your Breath Away

You and I are able to offer a sacrifice to God only through our confession of Jesus as our Savior. Your sacrifice is like a fruit that comes from your lips, flowing from your heart. As your sacrifice of praise flows out, then you grow in wonder. Growing awe makes you gasp at His power. I hope I can always stand in awe of God when He moves in my life or the lives of those around me. I hope God's wonder will always take my breath away. I hope I'll never be so jaded by the rituals of my denomination or the doldrums of life that I fail to see the grace.

Remember, life is not measured by how many breaths you take in your lifetime, but how many times you are breathless with joy and praise.

How many times lately has life taken your breath away? Are you in the right places at the right times, as God leads you? May Jesus give you abundant grace, and may you have the courage to endure disgrace when appropriate, with every breath you take.

I Aim to Please

Here's one last command from Christian: "And do not forget to do good and to share with others, for with such sacrifices God is pleased" (Hebrews 13:16). What does this verse say you should not forget? Two things you probably learned in kindergarten: do good and share. You may be absolutely sure you should do as much good as you can, with all your heart, soul, mind, and strength (Mark 12: 30). Here is the promise: When you do the best you can to praise Him, to do good, and to share with others, God is pleased.

As God's words "Render unto Caesar" reminded me of my citizenship (Study 9), Christian reminds us, "Obey your leaders and submit to their authority. They keep watch over you as men who must give an account. Obey them so that their work will be a joy, not a burden, for that would be of no advantage to you" (Hebrews 13:17). Christians please God when they are good citizens who help their government.

He also asks for prayer: "Pray for us. We are sure that we have a clear conscience and desire to live honorably in every way. I particularly urge you to pray so that I may be restored to you soon" (Hebrews 13:18–19).

Touch My Heart, Lord Jesus
O God of grace, who became a sacrifice for me, help me step outside the camp to serve You. Give me courage to bear disgrace, according to Your will, Your grace. Help me avoid false religion or false laws for living. Keep me from the world's aims; may I always aim to please You. May I do good, share, and pray, always standing in awe of You. Amen.

❧ FRIEND TO FRIEND ❧

How do your lips offer the sacrifice that pleases God?

If you know a song about offering a sacrifice of praise, sing it with your study partner.

STUDY 30 *"More Better"*—A Life of Grace
HEBREWS 13:20–25

A FAMOUS CAJUN CHEF, Justin Wilson, often said the dish was "more better" after he threw a handful of chili peppers in the mix. He usually ended, "I *garontee* it." When they first saw him, my family thought he had stolen our expression of "more better." For as long as I can remember, when we gather for a reunion, every dish is "more better," the new babies are "more better," and especially each new bride is "more better" than our relative who married her! What a heritage of laughter we have in our family!

Following World War II, jobs were scarce, and when my dad returned home from the war, he wasn't able to return to his former job, taken by someone else. For a while he drove a bus in our town. Sometimes my mother worked, and on those days, Daddy took us for a bus ride with him while he worked. The bus had no radio, and my dad loved music, so he'd stand my brother and me by the dash to sing for the customers. Clowning around, he'd say, "Ain't this more better than any radio?" One of the riders replied, seriously, "It's gooder than I ever heard!" Daddy immediately shared the remark with Mother and his sisters and brothers. Today all of us say "gooder," even though we know the correct word is "better" (at least, I think we know better).

Everything Good for Doing His Will
Christian, the Hebrews writer, ends with a blessing: "May the God of peace, who through the blood of the eternal covenant brought back from the dead our Lord Jesus, that great Shepherd of the sheep, equip you with everything good for doing his will, and may he work in us what is pleasing to him, through Jesus Christ, to whom be glory for ever and ever. Amen" (Hebrews 13:20–21).

This benediction pronounces that God, who brought Jesus back from the dead, will (1) equip you and (2) work in you. The most wonderful thing you can see on earth is a church that is acting out these words. As the Holy Spirit works in them, church members are equipped for service. "Now you are the body of Christ, and each one of you is a part of it" (1 Corinthians 12:27). "The body is a unit, though it is made up of many parts. . . . For we were all baptized by one Spirit into one body" (1 Corinthians 12:12–13).

Christian adds: "Brothers, I urge you to bear with my word of exhortation, for I have written you only a short letter" (Hebrews 13:22). Do you feel this study has been a long one? After spending weeks of study, it may seem long to you. However, God would urge you to read more of the Bible. We please God by further reading of His Word. This last study can be only a beginning. You may want to read *Friend to Friend: Enriching*

Friendships Through a Shared Study of Philippians and *Friendships of Purpose: A Shared Study of Ephesians*, or if God calls you to a mentor relationship as you study His Word, study *Woman to Woman: Preparing Yourself to Mentor*.

⊰ FRIEND TO FRIEND ⊰

What two things does Christian suggest that God will do?

1.

2.

If all of us are equipped to work together to please God, how does that work in a local church?

Do you attend a church where these two things take place?

Share with your study friend.

Inside the Prison

Then Christian shares good news: "I want you to know that our brother Timothy has been released. If he arrives soon, I will come with him to see you" (Hebrews 13:23). Timothy, who has been with Paul in prison, has been set free (as you have been set free from sin). God says, "The Spirit of the Sovereign Lord is on me, because the Lord has anointed me to preach good news to the poor. He has sent me to bind up the brokenhearted, to proclaim freedom for the captives and release from darkness for the prisoners . . . to bestow on them a crown of beauty instead of ashes, the oil of gladness instead of mourning, and a garment of praise instead of a spirit of despair" (Isaiah 61:1, 3). Do you feel God has anointed you to do any of these things? He calls each of us to do special things for Him.

Notice in Hebrews 13:23 that Christian hopes to visit the Jews to whom he's writing. How many times have you promised to visit and never got around to it? Maybe today is a time to act.

Step Outside Your Comfort Zone

How many prisoners do you know? We've talked a lot about disgrace and living outside the camp. We've even talked about how hard it was for the

Jews to leave their old laws and their established religion and live in faith. It's just as hard today, isn't it? You can wait to obey Him, delay serving Him, and never step out in faith. It's your choice—but it's not Jesus' way to stay in a comfort zone. He was willing to sacrifice, to praise, to pray, to serve in hard places. Just do it. Step outside your comfort zone.

Christian closes this letter reminding us of our Christian fellowship: "Greet all your leaders and all God's people. Those from Italy send you their greetings" (Hebrews 13:24). Since this study has been in letter form, you've seen a good example of communication among Christians. It might be called "communion with the saints."

Christian ends with a final communication: "Grace be with you all" (Hebrews 13:25). We ended Study 29 with a title for God: God of Grace. Grace is a title used for kings. Have you ever seen an old movie in which a citizen says, "Yes, your Grace," to the royal? Often our earthly royalty is far from perfect. Our perfect God is able to provide lasting peace and grace because He created them. As you end this study, may you have unending grace!

❧ FRIEND TO FRIEND ❧

How do you communicate with your friends?

• Through email
• By letter
• In short notes, cards
• Face to face
• By telephone
• On my cell phone
• In chat lines
• Through bulletin boards
• By Morse code
• Via telegram
• Through a prison chaplain
• Other:

When you communicate, do you . . .

• Scream and shout?
• Joke?
• Laugh and grin a lot?
• Hug?

- Always keep your language clean?
- Encourage them?
- Talk about God's will?
- Tell them about Jesus?
- Help equip them as Christians?
- Keep it short?
- Share good news?
- Bless them with God's grace?

Have you ever seen an old movie in which someone was addressed as "Your Grace"?

What was the character of that king, queen, or other royalty?

How did that character differ from God?

If you know the words to "Amazing Grace," sing it now with your study friend.

Congratulations! You have now completed a study of one of the most complex books of the Bible—a study of Jewish and Christian history, Old Testament and New Testament doctrines, and character studies of people from the prostitute Rahab to Melchizedek, the unique foreshadowing of Jesus Christ! Yet there is so much more we could have covered! My prayer is that this Bible study has enriched you and equipped you with understanding to serve God "more better."

✣ FRIEND TO FRIEND ✣

List here two important truths God has taught you as you have studied Hebrews.

Share these (and others, if you have time) with your study friend. Give each other a high five and pat each other on the back for a job well done!

Touch My Heart, Lord Jesus
God of peace and grace, equip me with everything good for doing Your will. Bless me and make my life pleasing to You, O my God. Help me encourage others, as Your Word in Hebrews has encouraged me. May I step outside my comfort zone to communicate and share Your wonderful love. To You be praise and glory forever! Amen.

As your conclusion to this study, take turns reading the poem at the beginning of Study 6 or Study 28 (your choice). End with prayer together.

Use the QR reader on your
smartphone to visit us online at
newhopedigital.com

If you've been blessed by this book, we would like to hear your story. The publisher and author welcome your comments and suggestions at: newhopereader@wmu.org.

Get more out of your reading experience
with free book club guides, small-group study guides,
and more at NewHopeDigital.com.